FATHER, FRIEND, *and* JUDGE

DESTINY IMAGE BOOKS BY ROBERT HENDERSON

FATHER, FRIEND, *and* JUDGE

THREE DIMENSIONS OF PRAYER THAT RECEIVE ANSWERS FROM HEAVEN

ROBERT HENDERSON

DESTINY IMAGE® PUBLISHERS, INC.

P.O. Box 310, Shippensburg, PA 17257-0310

"Promoting Inspired Lives."

This book and all other Destiny Image and Destiny Image Fiction books are available at Christian bookstores and distributors worldwide.

Cover design by Eileen Rockwell
Interior design by Terry Clifton

For more information on foreign distributors, call 717-532-3040.

Reach us on the Internet: www.destinyimage.com.

ISBN 13 TP: 978-0-7684-5089-7
ISBN 13 eBook: 978-0-7684-5165-8
ISBN 13 HC: 978-0-7684-4317-2
ISBN 13 LP: 978-0-7684-5166-5

For Worldwide Distribution, Printed in the U.S.A.
1 2 3 4 5 6 7 8 / 24 23 22 21 20

CONTENTS

ENDORSEMENTS

We are in the season of greater revelation of God, the Father. When you understand His true nature, watch how quickly our righteous judge answers your prayers.

SID ROTH
Host, *It's Supernatural!*

Father, Friend, and Judge is a masterful contemporary reimagining of the path, progress, and purpose of the Christian life through the lens of the author's experience kneeling in prayer and standing in the courtrooms of heaven. Robert Henderson has combined a wealth of biblical insight with vast personal experience to frame a truly Christian world view that will challenge many traditional/historical approaches to God and open new doors to glorious encounters with Him. This book can change your life. Read it prayerfully and be prepared to discover many new spiritual dimensions in your walk with God.

JOAN HUNTER
Author/healing evangelist
Host, *Miracles Happen!* TV show

As I read the manuscript of Robert Henderson's new book, *Father, Friend, and Judge*, it became clear to me that this is no ordinary book—it belongs in a class all by itself. Robert Henderson has taken revelation that he has received concerning dimensional truths and has loaded them into the pages of this book as rocket boosters. Each chapter lifts us from the gravitational pull of limited thinking and preconceived notions into orbits of celestial grandeur! When

I finished the manuscript, I immediately wanted to get alone with God and seek Him. I believe you will as well.

JOHN KILPATRICK
Founder and Senior Pastor
Church of His Presence
Daphne, Alabama

Robert Henderson's book *Father, Friend, and Judge* made a huge impact on me. If you are hungry to know God and to experience Him in deeper ways, then this book is a must read! To give you a fore-taste, Robert pens, "God as Father brings us into the secret place, and approaching Him as Friend opens the Council of the Lord; coming before Him as Judge gives us access into the Courts of Heaven." *Father, Friend, and Judge*—thank you Robert Henderson!

PATRICIA KING
Author, Christian minister, television host

Psalm 65:4 begins with, *"Blessed is the man You choose, and cause to approach You, that he may dwell in Your courts."*

Many people are good Christians and may have been serving God for a long time. They do everything right, are obedient, and love the Lord. Although God does allow different circumstances into lives to prune and to teach, there are certain areas where no matter how much these people pray, they can never seem to see justice.

The psalm goes on to say, *"We shall be satisfied with the goodness of Your house, of Your holy temple."* Robert Henderson's teaching on the Courts of Heaven first allows us to see our identity in God. Knowing your identity will open your eyes to the difference between mercy and justice. From that point, you can approach the Courts armed with truth to receive justice and be satisfied with the goodness of God's house. You will learn to see God as a Father, a Friend, and a Judge, understanding how He functions and relates with us in each of these realms.

Robert's teachings personally changed my life. By applying his principles in a land issue I had, I saw immediate change! Saints, implement the teachings in this book for breakthrough and justice.

REVEREND BETTY KING
Betty King International Ministries

This book is foundational concerning our identity as believers and critical concerning our prayers as intercessors. Robert Henderson not only shares powerful revelatory insights from scripture, he shares inspiring examples of those who have experienced radical transformation through a greater understanding of God as *Father, Friend, and Judge*. This book not only provides strategic information for effective prayer, it is a powerful training tool for those who have answered the call to bring heaven to earth.

WANDA ALGER
Field correspondent with Intercessors for America
Five-fold prophetic minister
Author of five books, including *Prayer That Sparks National Revival* and *Moving from Sword to Scepter*

When I was in Heaven, I saw the Throne Room with our heavenly Father seated in majesty. Jesus, the Son of God was seated at His right hand in the glory. At that moment, I was home in this sacred place where justice and righteousness ruled. I saw Jesus, my Savior and the Judge of all existence, in the courts of Heaven. My friend Robert Henderson, in his book *Father, Friend, and Judge,* gives you understanding into how to engage our heavenly Father. You will gain clarity into the character and ways of the One who hears and answers your heartfelt requests in prayer.

DR. KEVIN L. ZADAI
Founder and President of Warrior Notes School of Ministry
Kevinzadai.com
Warriornotesschool.com

FOREWORD

ROBERT HENDERSON HAS WRITTEN THIS AMAZING BOOK of prayer secrets in simple, unpretentious terms for anyone who desires to learn to pray accurately and effectively. We are living in tumultuous times, and God has been preparing a people who will submit to Him as participants in His plan for mankind. Our prayers will avail much when we learn to pray as Jesus taught us, *"Our Father, dwelling in the heavenly realms, may the glory of your name be the center on which our lives turn. Manifest your kingdom realm, and cause your every purpose to be fulfilled on earth, just as it is fulfilled in heaven"* (Matt. 6:9-10 TPT).

Your view of God will determine your prayer life. Even though I grew up in a home where prayer was practiced every day and even witnessed miracles, I did not know God personally! I was born again at the age of twelve and was greatly relieved that I was not going to hell, but only if I could keep all the rules. Incidentally, I got saved many times. I decided that when I grew up, I would join a church that believed in once saved always saved, only to discover they called it *rededication*. I simply did not know God as a loving Father. It never occurred to me that He would be a Friend, and to think of Him as Judge was simply too frightening! Prayer was something my mother and daddy did, but it was not on my radar, and when I did pray it was an attempt to get God to do something for me or my family. I understand when people tell me they would pray if they knew how to pray. If you are one of these people, read the book!

It was an overcast January day when my kitchen turned into a brown, crusty field. In the distance I saw a man who began to plow row after row, and I met the Heavenly Plowman with tears running from my eyes. He deposited in me an insatiable desire to read the Bible, which became my prayer book. Later, He revealed the importance of the plowed ground. If God would reveal Himself to a miserable, unhappy housewife and mother of four, I knew that He could and would do this for anyone. In the beginning it was me and Jesus. I sat at His feet where I learned about the Father and the Holy Spirit. Before I would call, He would answer. Mysteries were unveiled.

After studying the subject of prayer for over forty years, I have come to understand there's always more to learn. When you desire truth in the inward parts, God will share those secrets that are found in His presence. Thank you, Brother Robert, for sharing the revelations you have received from God on prayer. The Holy Spirit will impart these revelations to the reader.

In this book by Robert Henderson, God unveils the revelation of wisdom and imparts spiritual understanding that is needed to pray in three dimensions. When you use these prayer strategies, your prayers will be transformed from soulish prayers led by circumstances that jerk us around to spiritual prayers led by the Holy Spirit. There is no greater prayer of agreement than praying in the three dimensions with the two prayer partners who cannot fail—Jesus and the Holy Spirit who know the mind of God. Your prayer adventure becomes exciting, not burdensome! The more you pray, the more you will desire to pray. It's all by His grace!

Today we are living in a strange, mixed-up, confused, deranged world! I am not surprised that things prophesied in the Scriptures are happening. I am surprised that I'm living here on planet Earth when good is called evil and evil called good—watching intelligent people set aside their common sense. The doctrines of demons are blanketing society with a great delusion and unfortunately sometimes invading the church. We cannot ignore the events of the day.

HOW THEN DO WE PRAY?

The secrets found in this book reveal three dimensions of prayer, Father, Friend and Judge, and reveal how you can step into any of the three. Even as darkness is blanketing the world, heaven's kingdom is being proclaimed all over the world, providing every nation with a demonstration of the reality of God. Jesus reveals, *"And after this the end of this age will arrive"* (Matt. 24:14 TPT). God is calling the Body of Christ to arise as participates in His plan for mankind. It's a time when the church will shine brighter and brighter even unto the noonday sun.

We are here at this time in history and have the privilege of being participates in the move of the spirit, praying for all nations. We can learn to pray with accuracy so the Father's kingdom will come and His will be done on earth as it is in heaven that He may be glorified.

One of my prayers is that the glory of the knowledge of the Lord will cover every nation from border to border, from sea to sea.

Praying opens the door for experiences, which must be supported by scripture. In this book, Robert Henderson unravels the mystery of prayer, taking us into the Secret Place of the Most High—our Father, Friend, and Judge. These three dimensions of prayer prepare us to pray effectively and see the glory of God. When you read about Brother Henderson's experiences in the three dimensions, do not skip over the scriptures, which are the foundation of prayer. Expect to be shifted into spiritual realities that will bring transformation in your everyday, stay-at-home, going-to-work life. Each time before you begin to read, bind your mind to the mind of Christ and allow the Holy Spirit to share spiritual secrets that will become your spiritual reality.

The blood of Jesus gives us access into the Secret Place and the Council of God where you learn vital prayer strategies. The God and Father of our Lord Jesus Christ adopts us as His sons and daughters and begins teaching, training, and disciplining us in righteousness. The first time I knew that my Father was chastising me, I wept because I had not been walking in truth. At the same time, I was overwhelmed by my Father's great love and mercy. He not only exposed my wrong perceptions and attitudes, He gave me the desire and power to do His good will and fulfill His purposes. My training had begun. I did not know at the time that He was calling me to a life of prayer that would become my life. I had an intense desire to obey Him and follow His direction.

Between the covers of this book you will learn how to function in the Courts of Heaven with confidence and the assurance that the Judge who is righteous and just will hear your petition. You have been raised up and seated in heavenly places in Christ Jesus, who is our Redeemer and Advocate, not only for us but also for this crazy, turned-upside-down world.

Choose to adopt these revealed prayer secrets and join a host of people who know their God, who identify with Christ and know the devices of the devil. *"If then you were raised with Christ, seek those things which are above, where Christ is, sitting at the right hand of God. Set your mind on things above, not on things on the earth"* (Col. 3:1-2).

Ask the Holy Spirit to open the eyes of your understanding. You have the mind of Christ, and you can trust the Holy Spirit to direct you in approaching any one of the three dimensions—Father, Friend, and Judge. You will begin encountering and interacting with spiritual activities by faith. Here in the presence of God you will learn to see, discern, and hold the very thoughts, feelings, and purposes of His heart. Will you commit to praying and not give up until heaven can penetrate and enter the earth realm? Everyone has a place in the dimensions of prayer! Let's get busy and be about our Father's business even as we live in two places at the same time—in the realm of the spirit and here on earth surrounded by darkness. You are the light of the world! Fill the atmosphere with accurate, effective prayers ushering in the tremendous end-time harvest, and pray without ceasing!

GERMAINE GRIFFIN COPELAND
Author of the *Prayers That Avail Much* book series

INTRODUCTION

PRAYER HAS BEEN THE MOST IMPORTANT PART OF MY spiritual life since 1980.

It was at this time that I fully surrendered to God's will for my life. From my earliest memory I have had an awareness of God. My family was religious, but we really didn't know God. In the earliest part of my childhood, we were a part of a very lifeless religious denomination. We came out of that group that my family had been associated with for at least 50 years or more. We then came into the Charismatic/Spirit-filled expression of the church. This was during the Jesus Movement days. Hundreds of thousands and even millions were coming out of stifled and stiff denominational churches. They were being swept up into the things of the Spirit and discovering that a whole new realm of God existed. The gifts of the Spirit were being revealed, and Jesus was unveiling Himself in great dimensions across cultures.

This movement that occurred in the 1960s, 1970s, and even into the 1980s changed the face of the church. We still see its impact across the boundaries of different groups. What people believe has shifted. Worship within groups that once stood against the movement I am describing now embrace *our music*. Even the way service times were ordered was impacted by this move of God that touched the church and culture. I was 12 years old when my family encountered this expression of the life of the Spirit. We as a family would never be the same and neither would I individually. Life was altered forever.

My father, Welton Henderson, became very hungry for God. He was in his mid-50s and developed this hunger to know God. He would sit up all night for two nights and read the Bible through. He would then sleep on the third night. He held this schedule for some weeks and months all the while holding down his full-time job as a surveyor. My mother, Mary Henderson, became very concerned about his behavior. In the denomination we were a part of, you were considered *lost* and going to hell if you left the church and did not attend. My dad had stopped going to the services and was talking of leaving the church altogether. This meant my dad would go to hell based on the belief of our church.

My dad then told my mom something that would rock our world. He announced after all the time of reading the Bible, "I am going to find myself a Pentecostal church." This was heresy. What we didn't know was that my sister, who is 18 years older than me, and her husband had already been swept into this Charismatic renewal that I have described. When they heard the conclusion my dad had reached, they suggested we should come and see what this was all about. The result was we made the move from the denominational expression of the church to this expression of the Spirit-filled one. To say this was life-changing is an understatement. We were transformed. We all were *baptized in the Holy Spirit and spoke in tongues.* The *gifts of the Spirit* begin to operate in and through us. More than anything, however, we fell in love with Jesus! Almost all the family, young and old, lived with an excitement of this new life and world we had discovered through the power of the Spirit.

The reason I am relating this is because it is a crucial piece to my story concerning prayer. Remember, this was transpiring when I was 12 years old. As I fast-forward to my early 20s, I am now married to my high school sweetheart, Mary. We had our first of six children born to us. Even though I had an awareness of God from my earliest years and had experienced many different encounters with the Lord, I was now uninterested in anything to do with ministry. I am saying this because I knew—and all who knew me understood—I was destined to be in the ministry and preach the Word of God. I had in fact preached my first message at 13 years old. Still, even though I wasn't backslidden in the classical sense, I had decided to do my own thing. Mary and I had charted our course and determined she would be a teacher and I would be a coach. We were preparing to go to school to move in this direction. It was at this point that God interrupted these plans and our life.

It was a normal day. I had worked all day. We needed bread and milk, so I was going to the convenience store. It was no more than a five-minute drive. Little did I know those five minutes were about to change the course of our lives. As I was driving, suddenly I became aware that God had entered my car. What I mean is His presence was there. I had not invited Him nor was I seeking Him. He was just there. I then heard these words: *"The time is drawing near for you to do My work."* It wasn't an audible voice, but it was clear, plain, and sure. I knew it was God.

I responded to these words with some of my own. I said, "Why now, Lord?" What I meant was I had responsibilities. I had a wife, a child, a house to pay for, and all the other duties associated with these. It didn't seem feasible or practical to be talking about such a thing.

Without hesitation, the *voice* came back with, "Because now you have to trust Me." I was rocked. I tried to resist for a little while, but it was useless. The Lord in His mercy and kindness worked in my heart to bring me to the place of surrender. He does this according to Philippians 2:13: *"For it is God who works in you both to will and to do for His good pleasure."* The Lord changes the desires to agree with His will and His pleasure. This is exactly what He did with me.

In a very short period of time, the thing I did not want to do, which was ministry, I began to ask the Lord to allow me to do it. This passion and desire has never left me for almost 40 years. He captured my heart with His love and purpose.

As this transpired, I immediately felt a *call to pray.* It was as if God was saying to me, "The first thing I am going to teach you is how to pray." No one I knew had the kind of prayer life I was feeling called to. We prayed at our meals, maybe whispered prayers under our breath at times, and prayed for a few moments at church, but this was all I knew. I was now, however, feeling this call to spend *time* in prayer. I didn't have the first clue how to do it. Having a heart to obey, I would go into our bedroom, shut the door, and determine to pray for an hour. I would begin to pray and ask God for things. I would think surely it had been 45 minutes. I would look at the clock and discover it had been seven instead. I knew I was in for something I knew nothing about.

As I did this every day, however, suddenly the presence of God would come into the room. Maybe it would take the major part of the prayer time, but *He* showed up. I found that the more I prayed, the quicker His presence would come. This began to change my life. I now know I was creating an altar in the spirit where my sacrifice was being accepted. We can see this when Abraham built an altar at Bethel in his day. Genesis 12:8 shows him building this altar:

> *And he moved from there to the mountain east of Bethel, and he pitched his tent with Bethel on the west and Ai on the east; there he built an altar to the Lord and called on the name of the Lord.*

We also see Abraham, or Abram as he was known at this time, returning to Bethel and this altar again in Genesis 13:3-4:

> *And he went on his journey from the South as far as Bethel, to the place where his tent had been at the beginning, between Bethel and Ai, to the place of the altar which he had made there at first. And there Abram called on the name of the Lord.*

In this place of this altar, Abram called on the name of the Lord. Later, we see something very significant happening in this place called Bethel. Jacob, the grandson of Abraham, encountered an *open heaven* in this very place. Genesis 28:10-19 describes the encounter Jacob had at this place:

> *Now Jacob went out from Beersheba and went toward Haran. So he came to a certain place and stayed there all night, because the sun had set. And he took one of the stones of that place and put it at his head, and he lay down in that place to sleep. Then he dreamed, and behold, a ladder was set up on the earth, and its top reached to heaven; and there the angels of God were ascending and descending on it.*

And behold, the Lord stood above it and said: "I am the Lord God of Abraham your father and the God of Isaac; the land on which you lie I will give to you and your descendants. Also your descendants shall be as the dust of the earth; you shall spread abroad to the west and the east, to the north and the south; and in you and in your seed all the families of the earth shall be blessed. Behold, I am with you and will keep you wherever you go, and will bring you back to this land; for I will not leave you until I have done what I have spoken to you."

Then Jacob awoke from his sleep and said, "Surely the Lord is in this place, and I did not know it." And he was afraid and said, "How awesome is this place! This is none other than the house of God, and this is the gate of heaven!"

Then Jacob rose early in the morning, and took the stone that he had put at his head, set it up as a pillar, and poured oil on top of it. And he called the name of that place Bethel; but the name of that city had been Luz previously.

It is no accident or happenstance that Jacob encountered God at this place. The altar grandfather Abraham had raised up and sacrificed at had opened a gate or portal in this place. When Jacob comes to this place and sleeps, in his dream the heavenly realm touches him. The principle is this—when we spend time and sacrifice to erect an altar, it opens a gate in the spirit. This is why the more I spent time in prayer, the easier it was to encounter the presence of God. My sacrifice before the Lord and calling upon His name opened a gate in the spirit world. To this day, when I pray I am most of the time instantly in His presence. The reason for this is I erected an altar in the spirit realm that has a gate open perpetually.

Many years later, I now have a greater understanding of what is occurring as I pray. You will notice the terminology I used to describe what would happen as I pray. I said *He showed up* or *His presence would come.* I no longer think this way. Even though I have encounters with the Lord as I pray, I don't think it is because He decides to show up. I now believe it is because I am stepping into a spiritual dimension through prayer. This is much more a New Testament concept. The apostle Paul declared that we are seated with Jesus in a spirit dimension. Ephesians 2:6 proclaims this important idea:

> *And raised us up together, and made us sit together in the heavenly places in Christ Jesus.*

This is not just religious talk. This is Paul describing a spiritual reality. At the same time that we are walking in the natural realm of this world, we can also be in another place in the spirit. I tell people all the time, I may have my feet on this floor or ground, but in the spirit I am seated in a throne of government with Jesus. This is what I mean when I say I am stepping into a spiritual dimension when I pray. It is not that His presence comes to me as much as it is that I am stepping into a spiritual realm where there is all sorts of spiritual activity. When I realize this, I can learn to cooperate with what is happening in this realm and see breakthrough come.

We are going to delve into this idea throughout the remainder of this book. We will discover that Jesus actually taught us how to enter three of these dimensions that His blood has made accessible for us. We will learn how to function in these places and see prayers be answered in unprecedented ways. These three dimensions are approaching God as Father, Friend, and Judge. Each one of these opens to us a spiritual realm where we encounter and interact with spiritual activities by faith. The result is the shifting of spiritual realities so what is in heaven can penetrate and enter the earth realm. This is why Jesus taught us to pray in Matthew 6:9-10 concerning getting what is in heaven into the earth.

> *In this manner, therefore, pray:*
> *Our Father in heaven,*
> *Hallowed be Your name.*
> *Your kingdom come.*
> *Your will be done*
> *On earth as it is in heaven.* (TPT).

Prayer is not trying to convince God to do something for us. Prayer is agreeing and working with God to shift things in the spirit realm so what is in heaven can come into the earth. We do this from the spiritual dimensions Jesus has granted us access into as a result of His death, burial, resurrection, ascension, positioning at the right hand of the Father, and the pouring out of the Holy Spirit. We have been granted the right to enter the holy of holies by the blood of Jesus according to Hebrews 10:19.

> *Therefore, brethren, having boldness to enter the Holiest*
> *by the blood of Jesus.*

This is a spiritual dimension speaking of the place of His presence and glory where we encounter Him and the spiritual activity surrounding Him. In these places we move with Him to see His passion fulfilled. We will continue to unveil these secrets and ministries in the coming chapter.

Get ready to experience new levels of glory and power as we learn to pray as Jesus taught His disciples.

CHAPTER 1

LIVING IN TWO PLACES AT ONE TIME

THE LORD DESIRES TO AWAKEN HIS PEOPLE TO NEW REALMS of the spirit. So often we have been what the Bible calls carnal. This isn't because we are bad people; it's just that we haven't been challenged past a certain place in our spiritual walk. Being carnal means we are ruled by our natural senses rather than the Spirit of God. It doesn't necessarily mean we are sinful or sinning. We are simply allowing the natural, seen realm more influence than the spiritual, unseen realm. If we are to overcome this, we must have our thinking changed. We must be aroused to the reality of this unseen dimension and learn to function there. This will require us learning to move in faith. The Bible is explicit concerning that which is unseen or spiritual. In Second Corinthians 4:17-18 this realm of the unseen is revealed:

> *For our light affliction, which is but for a moment, is working for us a far more exceeding and eternal weight of glory, while we do not look at the things which are seen, but at the things which are not seen. For the things which are seen are temporary, but the things which are not seen are eternal.*

Paul lets us know that what is seen is temporary while what is unseen is eternal. This is why it requires faith to operate and live with an awareness of what we cannot physically see. There is a real unseen world that actually is influencing and even controlling this seen world. We accept this and tap this realm through the avenue of faith. In Second Corinthians 5:6-7 we see again Paul's awareness of this reality:

> *So we are always confident, knowing that while we are at home in the body we are absent from the Lord. For we walk by faith, not by sight.*

Paul recognized a dimension in the spirit or heavenly realm that we cannot see naturally, yet it actually exists. He was certain of its existence and our future there. However, he also understood we can function in this unseen realm now. Colossians 3:1-2 gives us insight into this idea:

> *If then you were raised with Christ, seek those things which are above, where Christ is, sitting at the right hand of God. Set your mind on things above, not on things on the earth.*

Notice that Paul is exhorting us to seek what is above where Christ is seated with God. This is an unseen realm. Right now, we are to be going after things in the spirit dimension even though we cannot see them. This requires us to be spiritual and not carnal. We mustn't be afraid of such things, but realize we are actually made for this as new creations in Christ Jesus. We have access into this unseen realm through faith.

Years ago when our children were very small, one of our sons who was probably three or four years old was lying in his mother's lap. He began to tell Mary he didn't believe in Jesus because he *couldn't see Him*. Mary then began to tell him that even though he *couldn't see Him* with his eyes, he *could feel Him with his heart*. She was seeking to teach him that there is more than one way to *see*. We must also learn to see with our heart. We can be able to perceive with the heart what is happening in the unseen realm. Jesus showed His disciples that this is the way He functioned and did the miraculous. In John 5:19-20, we see Jesus giving them a secret to the signs and wonders He did.

> *Then Jesus answered and said to them, "Most assuredly, I say to you, the Son can do nothing of Himself, but what He sees the Father do; for whatever He does, the Son also does in like manner. For the Father loves the Son, and shows Him all things that He Himself does; and He will show Him greater works than these, that you may marvel."*

Jesus *saw* into the unseen realm and directed His actions in agreement with that dimension. When His actions on earth agreed with the actions in the heavenly realm, miracles occurred. Notice also that Jesus' ability to function in this was not from a gift. His ability was from an intimacy with the Father. Notice, however, that it was *the*

17

Father loving the Son that empowered Jesus to see. This is significant. It wasn't the love of the Son for the Father but the other way around.

We know that when we experience God's love it invokes from us an affection and devotion for God. This is what First John 4:19 clearly announces to us: *"We love Him because He first loved us."* We do love Him, but only from our encounter with His love for us. However, in John 5:20 where Jesus is revealing the key to His seeing into the unseen world, it was because the Father loved the Son.

It is the love of the Father that heals wounds, frees from condemnation, breaks the power of shame, and removes the effects of guilt. All of these bog down our spirit man so we cannot function in our true spirituality. The more we receive the love of the Father, the more our ability to live in two worlds at one time is activated. So seeing into the unseen dimensions of the spirit is not a result of a gift but an encounter with the love of the Father. The more we grow in intimacy and love of the Father, the more we will see into the unseen realm. Remember Paul's admonition in Colossians 3 to *set your affection on things above.* Spirituality is loving what is above more than what is beneath. As this possesses our hearts, we will see into these unseen realms more and more.

Many people think of themselves as not being spiritual enough or gifted enough to function in these places. Nothing could be further from the truth. As born-again people, we have capabilities we may not recognize we have. When we were born again, something much more happened than us just getting to go to heaven when we die. When we were born again, we were empowered to interact with heaven now! Heaven and the spirit realm became accessible to us now. This means we are now able to discern and agree with the activity of the spirit dimension. This is what Jesus was seeking to communicate to Nicodemus. This was one of the main ideas Jesus desired Nicodemus to grasp. John 3:13 during Jesus' discourse with Nicodemus unveils a powerful truth concerning this concept.

> *No one has ascended to heaven but He who came down from heaven, that is, the Son of Man who is in heaven.*

Many read this scripture and think it must be redundant. However, it is Jesus explaining what being alive in the spirit and born again grants. As the Son of Man and one functioning as a *man* in the earth, He ascended into heaven, came down from heaven, and is *presently in heaven.* He was not referring to what we traditionally would call heaven. He was referring to a heavenly realm where all sorts of spiritual activity occur. Jesus was seeking to get Nicodemus to understand that being born again wasn't about going to heaven when you die. Being born again was being able to step into heavenly or unseen realms now. Jesus was communicating that He wanted to help Nicodemus experience what He lived in. He was seeking to bring Nicodemus into the place of living in two dimensions at one time! Jesus wanted him to know that when his spirit man came alive as a mortal human being, he would no longer be limited to the natural. He would now have access and be awakened to the unseen realm of the heavenlies. We also see this in the life of Elijah. In First Kings 17:1 we see Elijah standing before King Ahab to proclaim judgment against him and the nation of Israel.

> *And Elijah the Tishbite, of the inhabitants of Gilead, said to Ahab, "As the Lord God of Israel lives, before whom I stand, there shall not be dew nor rain these years, except at my word."*

When I used to read this verse, I visualized Elijah in a time of prayer when he heard God speak to him about Ahab. I thought he then got up and went and spoke to Ahab as is recorded here.

However, when I read this passage more closely I noticed that Elijah didn't say "*before whom I stood*" but rather "*before whom I stand.*" In other words, it wasn't something he had done but rather was presently doing. He was standing in two places at one time. In the natural, he was standing before Ahab. In the Spirit, however, he was standing before the Lord God who lives. From this place in the spirit he was proclaiming judgment into the natural. The result was a fulfillment of the word that he spoke. We too as New Testament believers have the right, privilege, and responsibility to live in these two dimensions at one time. We can function from the spirit realm and change and alter things in the natural for God's will to be done. This is a secret that Jesus was seeking to communicate to Nicodemus. As New Testament born-again people, this can and should be our experience.

If we are to really get this idea and began by faith to function here, we need to understand some of Jesus' words perhaps from a new perspective. For instance, in John 14:2-3 we see Jesus talking about *mansions.*

> *In My Father's house are many mansions; if it were not so, I would have told you. I go to prepare a place for you. And if I go and prepare a place for you, I will come again and receive you to Myself; that where I am, there you may be also.*

This traditionally has been thought to be about each of us having this amazing house in heaven that we will live in after we die. If there is a literal mansion for me in heaven, I will take it. However, when I look at this scripture it seems this isn't what Jesus was referring to. First of all, Jesus talks about the *Father's house.* This is a reference to where God lives. He lives in the spiritual or heavenly dimension. Solomon spoke of this in First Kings 8:26-27. In his prayer of dedication of the temple he had built, he acknowledges the limitlessness of God.

And now I pray, O God of Israel, let Your word come true, which You have spoken to Your servant David my father. But will God indeed dwell on the earth? Behold, heaven and the heaven of heavens cannot contain You. How much less this temple which I have built!

Solomon understands that there is no house that can be built to hold God. He in fact dwells in the heaven of heavens, and this is too small for Him. God is dwelling and living in the spirit realm. So when Jesus refers to the Father's house He is referring to a dimension in the unseen realm in which God dwells and functions. In this realm, there are many mansions. The word *mansions* is the Greek word *mone,* and it means a place to stay. It can refer to the act of staying or the place being stayed in itself. In my estimation it is speaking of a dimension of the Spirit we presently have access into. It is not talking about a glorious house for us in heaven after we die. It is speaking of a place in the heavenly realm we presently can occupy and function from.

The word *mansion* carries with it the idea that it is a place of residence. In other words, there is a place in the spirit where we have rights and where we belong. It becomes a place of residence for us in the spirit. Some of my seer friends tell me that once you have been to a place in the spirit, you can go back there. They are communicating this idea. God grants us places in the spirit from which we can function. Just like with Elijah, things occur in the natural because of the place we occupy in the spirit dimension.

Please notice as well that Jesus speaks of *preparing a place.* Again traditionally this has been thought to mean a place in heaven for after we die. Jesus also says that if this place is prepared, He will come again and receive us to Himself. This has in my estimation confused believers. This is not talking about going to heaven when we die. It is speaking about a spiritual dimension available to us now. For instance, the whole idea of Jesus preparing a place for us is about what He would accomplish through His atoning work. As a result of His work on the cross, resurrection, and ascension a realm of the spirit would be made available to us previously only available to a select few—the prophets of the Old Testament. Prior to Jesus' coming only a handful of prophets had access into these spiritual dimensions. However, Jesus' death changed everything. This is why Acts 2:16-18 is such an important statement.

> *But this is what was spoken by the prophet Joel:*
> *"And it shall come to pass in the last days, says God,*
> *That I will pour out of My Spirit on all flesh;*
> *Your sons and your daughters shall prophesy,*
> *Your young men shall see visions,*
> *Your old men shall dream dreams.*
> *And on My menservants and on My maidservants*
> *I will pour out My Spirit in those days;*
> *And they shall prophesy."*

God promised prophetic abilities to everyone as a result of Jesus' death, burial, and resurrection and then the coming of the Holy Spirit. I believe this is what Jesus meant when He said *I will come and receive you to Myself that where I am you may be also.* He wasn't talking about His second coming but rather Him coming in and through the person of the Holy Spirit. John 14:16-18 shows that the coming of the Holy Spirit, our Comforter was actually Jesus coming to them again.

> *And I will pray the Father, and He will give you another*
> *Helper, that He may abide with you forever—the Spirit*
> *of truth, whom the world cannot receive, because it*
> *neither sees Him nor knows Him; but you know Him,*

for He dwells with you and will be in you. I will not leave you orphans; I will come to you.

Through the ministry of the Holy Spirit Jesus returned to us. Through the Holy Spirit we are able to be *with Him where He is.* The Holy Spirit empowers us to be prophetic so we can step into these spiritual realms now made accessible to us. We would all be able to function prophetically, not just a handful of select prophets. Jesus' work on the cross caused the veil between heaven and earth to be rent. Matthew 27:50-51 gives this account.

And Jesus cried out again with a loud voice, and yielded up His spirit. Then, behold, the veil of the temple was torn in two from top to bottom; and the earth quaked, and the rocks were split.

The heavy, thick veil in the temple that kept everyone away from the glory and presence of the Lord, except one man once a year, was ripped open. Suddenly what had been inaccessible since the fall of man in the Garden of Eden was now available again. Jesus' cry from the cross caused the ripping to occur. Man now had access to God again. The Holy Spirit coming on the Day of Pentecost was the anointing and empowerment to function in this newly acquired dimension of the Spirit. What only a few had been allowed to penetrate, all flesh could now prophetically function in and from. Wow! Jesus passed through the heavens according to Hebrews 4:14.

Seeing then that we have a great High Priest who has passed through the heavens, Jesus the Son of God, let us hold fast our confession.

He has taken His place as our High Priest speaking on our behalf in the Courts of Heaven. The office of High Priest is the highest judicial function in heaven other than God the Judge of All (see Heb.

12:23). Jesus passed through the heavens, which would mean the first heaven, second heaven, and into the third heaven. The first heaven is the atmosphere right above us. The second heaven is the place where principalities and powers function over territories in the earth (see Eph. 6:12). The third heaven is God's throne. Paul spoke of accessing this realm. Second Corinthians 12:1-4 tells the incredible words of Paul and what most consider his own experience.

> *It is doubtless not profitable for me to boast. I will come to visions and revelations of the Lord: I know a man in Christ who fourteen years ago—whether in the body I do not know, or whether out of the body I do not know, God knows—such a one was caught up to the third heaven. And I know such a man—whether in the body or out of the body I do not know, God knows—how he was caught up into Paradise and heard inexpressible words, which it is not lawful for a man to utter.*

Paul was allowed to see things in this heavenly dimension. The experience seemed to have left him confused as to whether he was in his body or temporarily was taken from his body. All he knew was he saw and experienced glories he seemed to have no words to describe. This was available to Paul and us because of all Jesus has done.

Jesus passing through the heavens is significant in that the work He did on the cross legally defeated the powers of darkness. They could no longer from the second heaven keep what was in earth out of heaven and what was in heaven out of earth. As Jesus *passed through the heavens,* He executed into place His legal work on the cross. The powers of darkness were rendered powerless to stop Him. He ascended all the way to the Throne of God where He received from the Father the Holy Spirit and poured Him out on us. Notice what Acts 2:32-33 says about Jesus reaching the throne of God in the third heaven.

> *This Jesus God has raised up, of which we are all witnesses. Therefore being exalted to the right hand of God, and having received from the Father the promise of the Holy Spirit, He poured out this which you now see and hear.*

When the Holy Spirit came into the room on the Day of Pentecost, three things were now apparent. First, what Jesus had done on the cross was the legal mandate that was now met. The powers of darkness' legal rights were revoked and removed because of what Jesus had done. Otherwise the Holy Spirit or promise of the Father would not have arrived. Second, Jesus had clearly reached the throne of God because He was now pouring out the Holy Spirit on them. Jesus was now seated as Lord of All. The coming of the Spirit said He had made it and was now rightfully placed and positioned. Third, the Holy Spirit was now upon these disciples to legally empower them to execute into place everything Jesus had died for. The Holy Spirit would continue the instructing process Jesus had begun. They would continue to learn how to step into these newly accessible realms of the Spirit and see God's purposes done through them in the earth. So much of what Jesus had taught them, they would now begin to understand and experience on a new level. They were continuing on their learning curve concerning spiritual dimensions and their ability to change life in the natural from the unseen realms.

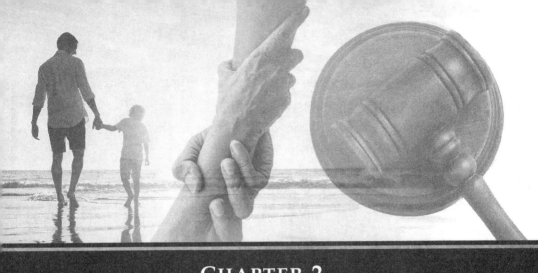

CHAPTER 2

PROPHETIC SENSES FOR HEAVENLY DIMENSIONS

I F WE ARE TO ACCESS THESE DIMENSIONS OF THE SPIRIT IT will take a developing of the prophetic abilities we now have in this New Testament dispensation. You have them, you just may not realize it. Hebrews 5:14 is explicit about our need to develop these abilities we have been entrusted with.

> *But solid food belongs to those who are of full age, that is, those who by reason of use have their senses exercised to discern both good and evil.*

When the Bible speaks of senses here, it is talking of the ability to prophetically discern. In other words, just like we have five natural senses, we also have prophetic abilities. These prophetic abilities give us the strength to function in this spiritual realm we have been called to and made for. Just like our five natural senses empower us to function in the natural realm, these prophetic abilities attached to our new nature we received when born again empower us to function in the unseen world. Remember, this is what Jesus was communicating to Nicodemus. Being born again wasn't about going to heaven when you die. Being born again was about functioning in heaven now. The problem is we haven't been sufficiently instructed in what became available to us when we were born again. As a result, we haven't lived in the fullness of what was intended and functioned in two worlds at one time.

We can see from the scriptures some ideas concerning our spiritual senses we now have available to us. The first step to functioning in them is to be aware of them. If there are five senses in the natural—touch, taste, sight, hearing, and scent—then there are at least these in the spirit realm. We can see these as they relate to the unseen realm we are called to function in. If any of the natural senses are disrupted or eliminated then it can result in us being classified as handicapped. For instance, if you are blind and can't see, you are considered disadvantaged and handicapped. The same is true for deafness and, to a lesser degree, the other areas of smelling, tasting, and touching or feeling.

The loss or interruption of any of these senses makes it more difficult to function in the natural realm. It is also true of the spirit dimension. Even though we may have a dominant way we perceive in the spirit world, we should have use of all the spiritual senses. The lack of any of them can result in us being handicapped in our movement and perception in the dimension we have been granted access

If then you were raised with Christ, seek those things which are above, where Christ is, sitting at the right hand of God. Set your mind on things above, not on things on the earth. For you died, and your life is hidden with Christ in God. When Christ who is our life appears, then you also will appear with Him in glory.

Our life, our purpose, and our reason for being alive on the planet are hidden in Christ with God. The more Jesus the Christ appears and becomes manifest, the more our life is revealed as well. Our purpose for being here is understood.

When Jesus said Nathanael was an Israelite indeed it meant he had been through the wrestlings of God and had become an "Israel." His ability to respond so quickly to the supernatural in Jesus was because of this purity of heart in him. Matthew 5:8 says the pure in heart will see God.

Blessed are the pure in heart,

For they shall see God.

Seeing God is not a reference to heaven and the afterlife. Seeing God is speaking of the ability to perceive in the spirit realm presently. The word *see* is the Greek word *optanomai,* and it means with eyes wide open beholding something remarkable. When we have a pure heart, we are enabled to *see* because there is nothing clouding our spiritual vision. We behold the beauty and glory of who Jesus is. We see with eyes wide open and stand amazed at Him.

There is a story I once heard that was told as a true account. There was this small boy of about two to three years of age. His father would walk in and catch him talking to *someone or something* he couldn't see. He would ask his son, "Who are you talking to?"

The boy would reply, "The angel."

This continued to happen and the dad became concerned. He began to wonder if this was an angel from the Lord or something demonic. So the next time he found his son speaking to this unseen being, he said his son, "Ask the angel why I cannot see him."

The boy then said to the angel, "Why can my dad not see you?" The boy then said, "Oh," as this angel seemed to answer him.

The dad then said to his son, "What did he say?"

The boy replied, "He says you cannot see him because your eyes have beheld too much evil."

Wow! Even as I write this I want to declare to the Lord, "Please forgive me for the evil I have beheld. I repent, Lord, and ask for Your cleansing to purify my heart." The pure in heart shall see God. May the Lord bring us to purity that we may behold Him and His beauty in the Spirit.

SPIRITUAL HEARING

Another prophetic sense that allows us to function in the unseen realms is hearing. We see this operating in Philip in Acts 8:26-27. The angel of the Lord spoke and Philip heard.

> *Now an angel of the Lord spoke to Philip, saying, "Arise and go toward the south along the road which goes down from Jerusalem to Gaza." This is desert. So he arose and went. And behold, a man of Ethiopia, a eunuch of great authority under Candace the queen of the Ethiopians, who had charge of all her treasury, and had come to Jerusalem to worship.*

Philip left a revival God had used him to birth in Samaria because he heard a word from God through an angel. This was because of his sense of hearing in the spirit world. As he obeyed the word he heard, he went into the desert. He there encountered an Ethiopian in a chariot. The Spirit then spoke to him as this Ethiopian eunuch was passing by. Acts 8:29 says Philip heard not the angel this time but the Spirit of God.

> *Then the Spirit said to Philip, "Go near and overtake this chariot."*

The result was this Ethiopian was born again, baptized, and history tells us had great influence for the kingdom in the palaces of Candace. This all happened because Philip had the ability to hear in the Spirit realm.

Several years ago, I was on a mission trip to the nation of Belize. We were traveling through the interior of Mexico on a single engine private plane. We had landed and spent the night in a certain Mexican city. As we were preparing to fly the remainder of the way to our destination the next morning, I took the canteens we had in the plane inside the airport to fill them with drinking water. Remember, this was a single engine private plane with the pilot and co-pilot up front and two very small seats in the back. We were truly flying in luxury. There were no flight attendants, restrooms, meals, drinks, or other creature comforts available. Anything we thought we might want or need we had to take with us ourselves for the next several hour trip. This was why I was in the airport terminal getting water in a canteen.

As I filled the canteen and was on my way through the terminal and back to the plane, I glanced to my right and saw a man standing ready to board his plane. The moment I did, my heart leapt and I knew I was to talk to him about the Lord. I very quickly second-guessed myself, because I cannot speak Spanish. I kept walking, but looked over my shoulder toward him again. My heart and spirit again quickened and I *knew* I was supposed to speak to him.

However, because I was deep in the interior of Mexico and could not speak the language, this was confusing me. I kept walking. I looked one more time at the man as I got farther and farther away from him. Again, my heart jumped and it was as if I was *hearing* the Lord say, "Speak to this man about Me."

I knew I could not disregard this voice. To do so would be to be disobedient to the Lord. I then concocted a plan. I took my watch off and I would go up to him and ask in English what time it is. If he answered in English, I would know I was hearing the Lord. If he didn't speak English I would chalk it up to a vivid imagination and move on.

As I approached him, I said, "Excuse me, sir, could you tell me what time it is?" To my amazement, in perfect English he answered me and gave me the time. Now I was pretty confident that I was *hearing* the Lord. Now I needed to just figure out *why* the Lord wanted me to speak to this man. You should factor in that the people I was with on the flight to Belize were waiting for me at the plane. I needed to hurry or they were going to be worried or upset with me for delaying our departure—which in fact they were when it was all said and done. They didn't know I had been interrupted with a mission from the Lord.

As I stood before this Mexican man having broken the ice by asking the time, I then continued the conversation. I was running out of time and needed to get back to the plane. I didn't have time to hem and haw around. Whatever I needed to do with this man I needed to get done. Therefore, I just dove in and went for it! I asked him, "May I inquire if you are a Christian and know Jesus as your Savior?"

His response astonished me. He said, "I am a backslidden pastor and have lost all my peace. I am tormented with mental troubles. I am on the way to the United States for an appointment with a psychiatrist to try and find peace."

I was absolutely astounded by what was happening. Clearly, I had heard God and this was a divine appointment. I then told the man that the reason I approached him was because God told me to. I told him that all he needed to do was repent of his sins. God would forgive him, his mental issues would be resolved, and he would find the peace he was so desperately looking for. I then asked if I could pray for him. Right there in the airport terminal, I asked the Lord to heal and restore this man and make him an example of His grace. I asked that every demonic scheme against him would be dismantled and he would be restored to his place in God. I then left him and hurried back to my party and tried to explain my delay to them. This is a practical example of the *hearing* sense in the spirit realm.

SPIRITUAL TOUCH AND FEEL

Touching or feeling is another sense that we can use to navigate the dimensions of the spirit realm. In the Old Testament the priests would place their hands into the breastplate and *feel* the Urim and Thummim. Exodus 28:30 speak of the Urim and Thummim and it being over the heart of the priest.

> *And you shall put in the breastplate of judgment the Urim and the Thummim, and they shall be over Aaron's heart when he goes in before the Lord. So Aaron shall bear the judgment of the children of Israel over his heart before the Lord continually.*

In that the Urim and Thummim were over the heart, it speaks of our heart or spirit being influenced by it. In other words, we can *feel* in our heart the desire, passion, intent, and direction of the Lord. This was one of the purposes of the Urim and Thummim in the breastplate of the priest. Numbers 27:21 declares that Joshua would be directed and led by what the priest sensed from the Urim and Thummim.

> *He shall stand before Eleazar the priest, who shall inquire before the Lord for him by the judgment of the Urim. At his word they shall go out, and at his word they shall come in, he and all the children of Israel with him—all the congregation.*

Through feeling that which was in or over the heart, direction from the Lord could be deduced. We also see Saul, the first king of Israel, seeking direction through this means but being denied it because of his rebellion. First Samuel 28:6 says God would not speak to Saul through any means including this one through the priests' ministry.

> *And when Saul inquired of the Lord, the Lord did not answer him, either by dreams or by Urim or by the prophets.*

This was clearly one of the ways God spoke and directed His people. Through the realm of *touch and feel*, the desire of the Lord could be discerned. When we take this into the New Testament, we see this is one of the ways God through the Holy Spirit makes His desires known. Philippians 4:7 give us insight into the *feeling* sense.

> *And the peace of God, which surpasses all understanding, will guard your hearts and minds through Christ Jesus.*

Through peace or the lack thereof, we can discern what the future holds and any adjustments we should make. First of all, we should know that the peace of God cannot be manufactured. It alone must come from Him. So if we have peace about a decision or something happening it is because He is giving it. This is one of the main means I use to determine what is happening in the unseen realm. Notice that this peace is something that surpasses understanding. In other words, it may not make sense in the natural, but the Spirit of God is testifying that everything is okay. I can have a confidence because I have the peace of God about events and circumstances I am facing.

The Bible says this peace *guards* our hearts and minds. This word *guard* is the Greek word *phroureo*. It means to be a watcher in advance. It means to mount a sentinel and to post spies at the gate. Wow! So if I have peace about something even if in the natural it doesn't seem good, I can be confident things will move into divine order. The Holy Spirit is standing as a guard reporting to me that everything coming toward me is good and I have no need to worry. On the other hand, if everything looks good but the peace of God is absent, I must take the knowledge of this and make any adjustments necessary. Some of the times I have gotten into trouble were when I disregarded the lack of peace because things seemed right in the natural. I made a decision from my logic and lived to regret it because I dismissed the lack of peace I was *feeling*. This is the *feeling and touching* sense in the spirit realm. Colossians 3:15 gives us one more word about the peace of God and its operation in us walking in the unseen realm.

> *And let the peace of God rule in your hearts, to which*
> *also you were called in one body; and be thankful.*

The word *rule* is the Greek word *brabeuo* and it means to govern. In other words, we are to allow the peace of God to govern our decisions and lives. If we will pay close attention to the presence or absence of the peace of God, He will direct us and keep our steps from falling. We must give the peace of God the governing realm in and over our lives. Some have said that the peace of God with regard to governing our lives is like an umpire in a baseball game. It is what calls the balls and strikes and lets us know what is in bounds and what is out of bounds. If we will walk in such a way with an awareness of the presence or absence of God's peace, we will be able to navigate the unseen realm and its effect on the natural.

We see those in the early church operating by this sense. Acts 15:25 uses a phrase that would imply the leaders of the church paid attention to the peace of God in their decisions.

> *It seemed good to us, being assembled with one accord, to send chosen men to you with our beloved Barnabas and Paul.*

The phrase "it seemed good to us" could imply they had peace and it seemed right in the spirit to send these men to them. They allowed the peace of God to direct their decisions as it was necessary in leading these New Testament churches. We must learn to live under the constraints of the Spirit and be led by the peace of God. This is the whole *feeling and touching* sense in the unseen realms of the spirit.

SPIRITUAL SMELL

Another sense that helps us function in the unseen dimensions of the spirit is the sense of *smell*. There are a couple of ideas concerning this. First of all, I have literally experienced a natural smelling from things in the spirit. I remember in one service where a literal aroma of frankincense filled the room. It was supernatural in nature. It was not coming from a natural source. This was because the Lord and those who accompany Him in the spiritual realm had come into the room with the fragrance of their presence. When this occurs, we must know it is a sign of the presence of heavenly beings among us.

Song of Solomon 3:6 tells us the Bridegroom coming toward us carries a fragrance.

> *Who is this coming out of the wilderness*
>
> *Like pillars of smoke,*
>
> *Perfumed with myrrh and frankincense,*
>
> *With all the merchant's fragrant powders?*

The Lord and His glory comes with an aroma and fragrance that we can detect when we are sensitive. Lord, would You awaken this dimension of sensitivity to detect the glory of who You are and the aroma of Your glory.

When Mary anointed Jesus with the costly oil, the aroma of it filled the whole house in John 12:3.

> *Then Mary took a pound of very costly oil of spikenard, anointed the feet of Jesus, and wiped His feet with her hair. And the house was filled with the fragrance of the oil.*

Smelling a fragrance from heaven can be the result of an anointing coming into the room from heaven. It is very precious and costly. This is what I feel filled the room on that day when that strong sense of frankincense was there. Philippians 4:18 also speaks of our offerings creating an aroma.

> *Indeed I have all and abound. I am full, having received from Epaphroditus the things sent from you, a sweet-smelling aroma, an acceptable sacrifice, well pleasing to God.*

There can be offerings released that can create fragrances in the spirit realm that can be smelled in the natural. Our offering can actually release a sweet-smelling aroma that can be smelled naturally if we are sensitive to it. When we smell something in the spirit it can be a sign of what is occurring in that dimension. We should seek to develop these senses and be aware of that which is happening in the unseen realm. The Bible also says we as believers carry an aroma in the spirit. Second Corinthians 2:15-16 shows that in the spirit dimension our lives are carrying an aroma.

> *For we are to God the fragrance of Christ among those who are being saved and among those who are perishing. To the one we are the aroma of death leading to death, and to the other the aroma of life leading to life. And who is sufficient for these things?*

We are to be carrying the fragrance of the Lord among the lost and the saved. Whether we smell it naturally or not, it would seem our lives emit an aroma in the spirit world that is being smelled. It is speaking of the life and glory of the Lord on our lives. I guess the question might be, "What do we smell like in the spirit?" May we carry the aroma of the Lord. This is what Esther carried as she was prepared to come before the king. She had been anointed with oils and fragrances in preparation for her coming before the king. Esther 2:12 tells us that Esther and all who would go before the king to see if they would be chosen to be his wife had 12 months of purifying with sweet aromas.

> *Each young woman's turn came to go in to King Ahasuerus after she had completed twelve months' preparation, according to the regulations for the women, for thus were the days of their preparation apportioned: six months with oil of myrrh, and six months with perfumes and preparations for beautifying women.*

The fragrance of these women would reach the king before their actual presence did. They had been so perfumed that they carried an aroma designed to impress the king and cause them to be chosen. The Holy Spirit will anoint us with sweet perfumes that will cause the King to desire us. May we carry the aroma of heaven in the spirit world that causes us to be desired by the King Himself.

The other thing the realm of smelling speaks of is the ability to discern. For instance, anyone who could not smell was eliminated from functioning as a Levite in the Temple. Leviticus 21:18 tells us that, among other things, if a man had a deformity in his nose he could not function as priest.

> *For whatsoever man he be that hath a blemish, he shall*
> *not approach: a blind man, or a lame, or he that hath a*
> *flat nose, or any thing superfluous* (KJV).

The deformity of the nose speaks of the inability to potentially smell and discern. Smelling speaks of discerning in the spirit realm. When we smell something in the natural, we normally have a sense of what is producing that smell. We can tell through smell what is happening in the natural. The sense of smell alerts us to good things like apple pie but also to dangerous things like gas leaks. We can move based on what we smell and get the benefits of it. To function in the unseen dimension, we must have a smelling sense or ability to discern in the unseen realm as well. First Corinthians 12:10 speaks of the discerning of spirits.

> *To another the working of miracles, to another prophecy,*
> *to another discerning of spirits, to another different kinds*
> *of tongues, to another the interpretation of tongues.*

Among other gifts or manifestations of the Holy Spirit, discerning of spirits is mentioned. This is the ability to recognize the presence of angels, demons, and other spiritual forces seeking to influence a situation. It can also empower us to realize the motivation of a person. In other words, whether they are seeking to manipulate or are sincere in their motives, we can *smell* what is driving a person, thing, or circumstance. This can be invaluable because it will help us not to get tricked or deceived. Even Hebrews 5:14 again tells us that developing these prophetic senses can help us discern good and evil.

> But solid food belongs to those who are of full age, that is, those who by reason of use have their senses exercised to discern both good and evil.

The word *discern* is the Greek word *diakrisis*. It means judicial estimation. When we discern, we are making decisions like a judge would. We are evaluating that which is being presented to us through the senses of the Spirit and making decisions concerning it.

I was in Switzerland doing a conference on the Courts of Heaven for a prophetic company of people. The man leading this group, who is very prophetic, had watched me operate over the course of a few days. He said to me, "As I've observed you, I've concluded some things about you." He continued, "You pay attention to several different things in determining what is happening in the spirit world. I've watched you take what you see, hear, feel, and discern and then you decide what is happening in the unseen realm."

No one had ever watched me this closely to recognize this. I then told him, "This is exactly what I do. I seek to pay attention to everything that is happening in the spirit dimension and then conclude what my response and movement should be." This is *discerning*. This is *diakrisis*. I am making judicial estimations based on the evidence I am picking up from the spirit realm. This is what we do when we discern. We are sniffing out what is actually happening in the dimension of the spirit.

Another thing we should notice is we discern both *good and evil*. Through the realm of discernment, we can sniff out both good and evil. In other words, we can determine the heavenly realm operation and the operation of the evil realm. When it is the heavenly dimension, we come into agreement with it by our faith and actions. This allows heaven to manifest in earth. When it is the evil realm, we undo it and know how to revoke its legal right to have operation in the natural realm. To fully understand this we must realize that whatever is in the spirit dimension or unseen realm must have agreement with someone in the seen realm for it to come into place in the natural sphere. This is what Jesus was referring to when He spoke of *gates*. Matthew 16:18 speaks of gates.

> *And I also say to you that you are Peter, and on this rock I will build My church, and the gates of Hades shall not prevail against it.*

A gate is a place of entrance. For the spirit realm to have entrance into the natural there must be a gate that comes into agreement with it. This can be a person, an organization, or anything that allows the spirit realm access through it. Here Jesus is saying that the church will prevail against the gates of Hades. These are things in the natural that allow satanic influence to come through them into the seen realm. It is the job of the church to shut or close these gates through revoking their legal right to operate.

For instance, people who have gained a realm of influence allow the will of hell to be done in the earth. These people either need to be converted or removed from their place of influence. They are a gate being used by the satanic spirit realm to bring its influence into the earth. This can be true of organizations, agencies, and other groups. These gates must be shut to stop the right of evil to propagate itself in culture. These gates have the right to operate because someone in the natural has granted them legal access to come in. On the other hand, there are gates of righteousness that allow God's will and influence to be done in the earth. When Jacob encounters God at Bethel, he realizes he is in the gate of heaven. Genesis 28:17 calls it *the house of God, the gate of heaven.*

> *And he was afraid and said, "How awesome is this place!*
> *This is none other than the house of God, and this is the*
> *gate of heaven!"*

Jacob was prophetically describing what the church was to be. We as the house of God are to be a gate of heaven. In other words, heaven can enter and penetrate the earth through us as the gate of heaven. When we come into agreement with heaven, heaven can enter through us and impact the earth!

John 5:19 tells us that miracles entering the earth realm from heaven were a result of heaven and earth coming into agreement.

> *Then Jesus answered and said to them, "Most assuredly,*
> *I say to you, the Son can do nothing of Himself, but what*
> *He sees the Father do; for whatever He does, the Son also*
> *does in like manner."*

When Jesus saw what was happening in heaven, He became a gate for it to enter the earth. As a gate He simply did in earth what He saw happening in heaven. The result was miracles. Jesus as a gate in the natural gave heaven the legal right to enter earth by agreeing with it.

This is so powerful. So when we discern what heaven is doing, we agree with it and the supernatural impacts the earth. This is the power of discerning or sniffing out what is going on in the unseen realm.

SPIRITUAL TASTE

The last spiritual sense to mention is tasting. First Peter 2:1-3 says we should taste of the graciousness of the Lord.

> *Therefore, laying aside all malice, all deceit, hypocrisy, envy, and all evil speaking, as newborn babes, desire the pure milk of the word, that you may grow thereby, if indeed you have tasted that the Lord is gracious.*

When we eat of the sweetness and graciousness of the Lord we grow and mature in the Lord. We need to consistently be eating from His sweetness. Revelation 10:8-11 tells us of an angel instructing John to eat a little book.

> *Then the voice which I heard from heaven spoke to me again and said, "Go, take the little book which is open in the hand of the angel who stands on the sea and on the earth."*
>
> *So I went to the angel and said to him, "Give me the little book."*
>
> *And he said to me, "Take and eat it; and it will make your stomach bitter, but it will be as sweet as honey in your mouth."*
>
> *Then I took the little book out of the angel's hand and ate it, and it was as sweet as honey in my mouth. But when I had eaten it, my stomach became bitter. And he said to me, "You must prophesy again about many peoples, nations, tongues, and kings."*

As John eats the book, it is sweet in his mouth. This is because the word of God to nations is a sweet thing. The book eaten becomes bitter in his stomach. A bitter stomach can cause one to vomit or spew out of the mouth. This is speaking of the unction from which John will prophesy. Amos 3:8 says that the word of God spoken into our spirit creates an unction to prophesy.

A lion has roared!

Who will not fear?

The Lord God has spoken!

Who can but prophesy?

When there is a stirring in our spirit, it can't be relieved except we prophesy that word. This is what it means when the sweet word we have tasted becomes bitter in our stomach. Out of our innermost being we release the word of the Lord. It starts off, however, as being the sweetness of His word we have *tasted*. We taste and see that the Lord is good. Tasting the goodness of the Lord also speaks of us receiving revelation and enlightenment. First Samuel 14:27 records the occasion when Jonathan the son of Saul puts forth his rod and begins to eat honey from the ground. The result was his eyes were enlightened.

> *But Jonathan had not heard his father charge the people with the oath; therefore he stretched out the end of the rod that was in his hand and dipped it in a honeycomb, and put his hand to his mouth; and his countenance brightened.*

When Jonathan, who was not privy to Saul's legalistic requirement to not eat, partook of this honey, enlightenment came to him. In other words, he wasn't under religious restrictions. Therefore, he was free to partake of the goodness of the Lord. The result was a spirit of revelation came to him. When we eat of the goodness of the Lord and taste of His graciousness, there is an unlocking of revelation we can receive. It is because we have been freed by His goodness and kindness. Don't be put in bondage again to legalism and religious constraints.

These are the five senses in the spirit realm that help us maneuver the spiritual dimensions we can move into through prayer. The more we use them, the more we develop in them. The operation in the spirit realms will progressively mature.

CHAPTER 3

FAITH AND THE REALMS OF THE SPIRIT

IF WE ARE GOING TO FUNCTION IN THE DIMENSIONS OF THE spirit that Jesus taught us about it, will be through faith. Everything we do is by faith. This is very important. Otherwise we keep expecting the Lord to do something for us He's not going to do. Stepping into faith is essential to operating in the unseen realms of the spirit. This is what Peter did when he heard Jesus bid him come in Matthew 14:26-32.

And when the disciples saw Him walking on the sea, they were troubled, saying, "It is a ghost!" And they cried out for fear.

But immediately Jesus spoke to them, saying, "Be of good cheer! It is I; do not be afraid."

And Peter answered Him and said, "Lord, if it is You, command me to come to You on the water."

So He said, "Come." And when Peter had come down out of the boat, he walked on the water to go to Jesus. But when he saw that the wind was boisterous, he was afraid; and beginning to sink he cried out, saying, "Lord, save me!"

And immediately Jesus stretched out His hand and caught him, and said to him, "O you of little faith, why did you doubt?" And when they got into the boat, the wind ceased.

Peter didn't just step out of the boat; he stepped into the faith realm. Every time I read this account, I can't help but think of the old *Twilight Zone* series that ran on American TV in the 1960s. Rod Serling, the host, would open the show with a speech that would always speak of stepping into an alternate dimension he called the "Twilight Zone." This spoke of people who were having an experience in a realm other than what we would call the natural. In these dimensions supernatural things occurred that could not happen in normal, natural life. Even though we aren't stepping into the Twilight Zone, we are stepping into an alternate dimension where the supernatural is natural and the abnormal is normal.

This is what happened to Peter. When he stepped out of the boat and onto the water, he stepped into another dimension. Please notice that Jesus was not holding Peter up. By stepping out of the boat and onto the water at Jesus' invitation, Peter stepped into the same realm Jesus was in. The result was the ability to do what was impossible in the natural.

As long as Peter stayed focused on Jesus and His word of "Come," he walked on the water. However, the moment that he took his eyes off Jesus, he began to sink. His doubt pulled him out of this supernatural realm and back into the natural. The principle is that it is faith that allows us to step into and function from this dimension. If we are to step into these realms of the Holy Spirit, we must be willing to get out of the boat of comfort and familiarity and take a chance. We must put our feet on the water and seek to move into and from this realm of faith. Remember that we by *reason of use* exercise these senses of faith (Heb. 5:14).

We see Jesus functioning in this realm in other places. For instance, when the people became demonically inspired to throw Him over a cliff, Jesus just walked through the midst of them. Luke 4:28-30 records the wrath-filled people desiring to destroy Jesus.

> *So all those in the synagogue, when they heard these things, were filled with wrath, and rose up and thrust Him out of the city; and they led Him to the brow of the hill on which their city was built, that they might throw Him down over the cliff. Then passing through the midst of them, He went His way.*

When read casually, it's easy to miss that the same people who wanted to kill Jesus allowed Him to walk out of the midst of them. Perhaps a divine stupor came over them so they suddenly no longer had a desire to destroy Jesus. Maybe Jesus stepped into this dimension of the spirit world and went invisible and simply walked away from those who wanted to annihilate Him. This may seem impossible. Yet this is exactly what I am saying. There is a dimension of the spirit we access through faith. In this dimension things that are impossible in the natural realm are normal and possible in this realm. I also believe we see this when Philip was transported by the Spirit from one physical location to another. We see this is Acts 8:38-40. Philip at the bidding of the Lord preaches the gospel to the eunuch. We spoke of this earlier. However, an even greater and amazing thing happened to Philip after his obedience to the Lord.

> *So he commanded the chariot to stand still. And both Philip and the eunuch went down into the water, and he baptized him. Now when they came up out of the water, the Spirit of the Lord caught Philip away, so that the eunuch saw him no more; and he went on his way rejoicing. But Philip was found at Azotus. And passing through, he preached in all the cities till he came to Caesarea.*

As soon as Philip baptized this eunuch, he disappeared from the scene. He was there and then he was gone. I love what the scripture says to describe this. Philip was *found* at Azotus. In other words, the Spirit took him and deposited him in Azotus. He kind of materialized in another place. As a '60s and '70s kid I remember the old *Star Trek* show with William Shatner as Captain Kirk and Leonard Nimoy as Mr. Spock. In this series they had the ability to dematerialize and rematerialize in another location. They called it being *beamed up*. In one sense of the word, this appears to be what happened here. Philip was in another dimension where it was possible to physically be instantly in another place. This boggles the mind, but is very scriptural. We see this being referred to by the sons of the prophets when Elijah was taken into heaven. Second Kings 2:15-16 shows the sons of the prophets being aware that it was possible for the Spirit of the

Lord to relocate someone in the physical. When Elijah was taken to heaven, they thought perhaps this was what had happened to him and he needed to be looked for.

> *Now when the sons of the prophets who were from Jericho saw him, they said, "The spirit of Elijah rests on Elisha." And they came to meet him, and bowed to the ground before him. Then they said to him, "Look now, there are fifty strong men with your servants. Please let them go and search for your master, lest perhaps the Spirit of the Lord has taken him up and cast him upon some mountain or into some valley."*
>
> *And he said, "You shall not send anyone."*

These prophetic people were aware that it was possible to step into spiritual realms where these things could occur. It was an understood experience in the prophetic and spiritual realm they functioned in. Of course, in this case Elijah was not to be found because his disappearance was a result of him going to heaven. However, it does show the ability to step into a spiritual dimension where such things like this do happen. I am not suggesting that these things are commonplace. I do believe they are for today. I do believe we have become so carnal and ruled by our physical senses that we have cut ourselves off from these kinds of encounters. The more we can become spiritual and step into realms and dimensions of the Spirit, the more likely these things are to happen. The beginning place of these is to become sensitive to the spiritual realm. Should we ever be relocated by the Spirit, as He might deem necessary, we must first learn to walk in two dimensions as a normal expression of our Christianity.

If we are to move into these realms and function there, it requires faith. Hebrews 4:1-2 tells us that any word we receive we have to mix it with faith.

Therefore, since a promise remains of entering His rest, let us fear lest any of you seem to have come short of it. For indeed the gospel was preached to us as well as to them; but the word which they heard did not profit them, not being mixed with faith in those who heard it.

We are told we should fear that we would miss out on something God has for us. To get it, we must be willing to mix with principle faith the word we hear. If we are to move in the spirit realm, we must mix faith with whatever we perceive. Whether it is through seeing, hearing, smelling, feeling, or tasting, if we don't mix faith with it, we miss what God is saying. The children of Israel did not mix faith with the word they heard. Therefore, they did not move into the promised land and get their inheritance. They died in the wilderness because they didn't let faith arise in their hearts when they heard the word. I believe this is what Jesus was referring to in Matthew 13:14-16.

And in them the prophecy of Isaiah is fulfilled, which says:

"Hearing you will hear and shall not understand,

And seeing you will see and not perceive;

For the hearts of this people have grown dull.

Their ears are hard of hearing,

And their eyes they have closed,

Lest they should see with their eyes and hear with their ears,

Lest they should understand with their hearts and turn,

So that I should heal them."

But blessed are your eyes for they see, and your ears for they hear.

Ears that cannot hear and eyes that cannot see are referring to the absence of faith in the midst of spiritual perception. That even though they have the spiritual ability to perceive, there is no faith in their heart to move upon it. What a tragedy. The choice to not respond in faith to what we spiritually perceive locks us into a place of natural limitations. However, if we can mix faith with what we perceive, we can step into a bold new world where anything is possible. Jesus said that if our eyes see and our ears hear they are blessed and we are healed.

Supernatural healing is a result of awakening in our spiritual perception and mixing faith with what we perceive. Taking a step of faith based on what is happening in the spirit realm unlocks so much that removes limits from our lives. This is why God loves faith. Hebrews 11:6 tells us that God is pleased with faith.

> *But without faith it is impossible to please Him, for he who comes to God must believe that He is, and that He is a rewarder of those who diligently seek Him.*

It seems that faith excites the heart of God. If we want to get God excited, then become those who with childlike belief respond to Him. We shouldn't be those who have to be convinced. We should be those who choose to respond to what we pick up in the realm of the spirit. Jesus got excited when people had childlike hearts. Luke 10:21 says Jesus rejoiced in His spirit when people had childlike hearts that got exhilarated about the things of God.

> *In that hour Jesus rejoiced in the Spirit and said, "I thank You, Father, Lord of heaven and earth, that You have hidden these things from the wise and prudent and revealed them to babes. Even so, Father, for so it seemed good in Your sight."*

The word *rejoice* is the Greek word *agalliao,* and it means to jump for joy. In His spirit, Jesus was jumping for joy because His disciples were babes in their hearts. Wow! Jesus was thrilled that there were people who were getting it. They were excited and willing to move in faith at His word. Oh that the Lord would help us to be these kinds of people and receive revelation from the realms of the spirit.

This word *babes* is the Greek word *nepios,* and it means not speaking. In other words, it implies such a young person that they haven't even learned to talk yet. This tells us you don't need great spiritual maturity to move in the spirit realm. You simply need the simplicity of faith to just take God at His word. So often in Christian circles we have allowed our maturing process to remove faith from us rather than to develop it. Where is the one who will take the Lord at His word, learn to move in the spirit realm, and see the Lord manifested?

I remember hearing a very prominent leader in the Body of Christ tell the story of an encounter with an elder in a church he was a part of when he was a young believer. It seems that in the young believer was a great hunger for God. In his hunger for God, he expressed to this elder that he longed for all that God had for him.

The elder asked him if he had received the gift of tongues. His response was that he had. The elder then responded, "You have it all, then." The young man was devastated. He intuitively knew God had more than just tongues. He would not allow this elder's persuasion that this was all there was to quench his thirst for God.

This young man has gone on to be one of the most respected experts on the move of God and the flow of the Holy Spirit. His life has been a depiction of the presence and glory of the Lord. However, this exposes a problem we have in the church. Instead of atmospheres being created to produce hunger and thirst after God and encounters with Him, the opposite is true. Believing God is discouraged quite often as being foolish and ignorant. We have replaced faith with academics. Yet it has been those who have been willing to believe God and not scholars who change the world.

I remember standing on a platform after a very powerful service where God had manifested His power. People were healed, the prophetic had operated, and we had functioned from dimensions of the spirit realm. As I was dismissing the service after this time of glory, I heard the Lord clearly say, "You have seen but the edge of Me." I understood that the Lord was saying to me, "As good as you think this is, it is only a small part. Do not let yourself be satisfied. Keep believing Me and I will show you greater and more glorious things." I have sought to do this. If we are to move into the greater and more glorious dimensions of God, we must not allow ourselves to become religious and content. There must always be a holy hunger for the next places in God. This is what the apostle Paul sought to communicate in Philippians 3:13-15.

> *Brethren, I do not count myself to have apprehended; but one thing I do, forgetting those things which are behind and reaching forward to those things which are before I press toward the goal for the prize of the upward call of God in Christ Jesus.*
>
> *Therefore let us, as many as are mature, have this mind; and if in anything you think otherwise, God will reveal even this to you.*

Paul never considered himself to have arrived. He always was pushing for the next places in God. He actually said this was real maturity. Spiritual maturity is not exemplified by feeling like we have arrived.

Real spiritual maturity is always having this childlike heart that yearns for the next encounters and spheres in God and the spirit realm. If we can develop and maintain these passions, we can step into the dimensions of the spirit where the supernatural functions.

The critical key to operating in faith that allows us to access these spiritual dimensions is choice! If you will remember, when Thomas was not with the disciples when Jesus appeared to them, he refused to believe without seeing. John 20:24-25 records Thomas as saying he will not believe unless he can see.

> *Now Thomas, called the Twin, one of the twelve, was not with them when Jesus came. The other disciples therefore said to him, "We have seen the Lord."*
>
> *So he said to them, "Unless I see in His hands the print of the nails, and put my finger into the print of the nails, and put my hand into His side, I will not believe."*

Thomas doesn't say he can't believe; he says he will not believe. This means faith and believing is a choice. Jesus was gracious to Thomas and did manifest and show him a physical depiction of Himself. John 20:26-29 shows Jesus coming again and revealing Himself to Thomas. However, it wasn't without instruction and even a mild rebuke.

> *And after eight days His disciples were again inside, and Thomas with them. Jesus came, the doors being shut, and stood in the midst, and said, "Peace to you!" Then He said to Thomas, "Reach your finger here, and look at My hands; and reach your hand here, and put it into My side. Do not be unbelieving, but believing."*
>
> *And Thomas answered and said to Him, "My Lord and my God!"*

Jesus said to him, "Thomas, because you have seen Me, you have believed. Blessed are those who have not seen and yet have believed."

Jesus declared that Thomas' *need* to see Him physically in His resurrected state was second best. Those who believed without seeing were the absolute best. This is what is desired of us. When we simply *choose* to believe, this satisfies the heart of God. When we are able to process the spiritual unseen evidence presented to us and allow faith to arise, God is well pleased. Sometimes we can incorrectly think that God wants us to be a cynic and make Him have to prove Himself to us. This is what Thomas required. Jesus said to Thomas that he had cut himself off from a blessing of just operating by faith. Peter spoke of this in First Peter 1:7-8.

That the genuineness of your faith, being much more precious than gold that perishes, though it is tested by fire, may be found to praise, honor, and glory at the revelation of Jesus Christ, whom having not seen you love. Though now you do not see Him, yet believing, you rejoice with joy inexpressible and full of glory.

Notice that at the appearing and revelation of Jesus, faith will be rewarded. This is the faith that is operating even though we haven't seen Him, yet we believe. This faith when in operation produces in us inexpressible joy and glory. This is the faith we are to choose to walk in. We choose to pay attention to and value the unseen realm and the senses attached to it. When we do, we are ready to step into and function from the dimensions of the spirit that unlock the supernatural of the Lord in our world. We cast off the spirit of unbelief and choose to enter the adventure of faith. When we do, we enter a bold new world of the unknown. We move from just the natural, carnal realm to the unseen, spiritual dimension. Make that choice and step in!

Chapter 4

APPROACHING GOD AS FATHER

IN RESPONSE TO THE DISCIPLES' REQUEST TO BE TAUGHT TO pray, Jesus begins His discourse. He begins with what would famously be called *The Lord's Prayer*. It probably would better be called the model prayer because it was Jesus' initial teaching on how to pray. Regardless of how we would categorize it, Jesus was seeking to communicate spiritual truths concerning the realm of prayer. He begins by speaking of addressing God as *Father*. Another look at Luke 11:2 reveals a simple, yet profound truth.

> *So He said to them, "When you pray, say:*
> *Our Father in heaven,*

Hallowed be Your name.

Your kingdom come.

Your will be done

On earth as it is in heaven."

This alone would have been groundbreaking in that God being seen as Father would have been a familiarity not thought of in Jewish culture. The Jews' picture of God had been formed at Mount Sinai where they trembled at the revelation of God to them as a nation. Exodus 20:18-21 shows the people being terrified of God and His demonstration.

> *Now all the people witnessed the thunderings, the light-ning flashes, the sound of the trumpet, and the moun-tain smoking; and when the people saw it, they trembled and stood afar off. Then they said to Moses, "You speak with us, and we will hear; but let not God speak with us, lest we die."*
>
> *And Moses said to the people, "Do not fear; for God has come to test you, and that His fear may be before you, so that you may not sin." So the people stood afar off, but Moses drew near the thick darkness where God was.*

The people asked Moses to talk to God so they wouldn't have to encounter Him. Moses tried to calm them but they seemed petrified from the demonstration of God in the midst of them. Moses was even traumatized a bit it would seem. Hebrews 12:20-21 says that Moses was greatly afraid.

> *(For they could not endure what was commanded: "And if so much as a beast touches the mountain, it shall be stoned or shot with an arrow." And so terrifying was*

the sight that Moses said, "I am exceedingly afraid and trembling.")

This was the view they had of God as a nation of people. When Jesus began to introduce God as their Father, this was a foreign concept. The idea that God wasn't this distant, far-off, strict and demanding deity who exacted obedience or else, was shaking their concept of Him. The image of Him being a Father who loved, cared, provided, protected, and to whom they could approach in prayer from this realm was a new idea. They would come to understand that this was one of the main things Jesus came to unveil. This is why later Jesus would let it be known this was a major portion of His mission in the earth. John 14:9 reveals Jesus speaking to Philip and showing this truth.

> *Jesus said to him, "Have I been with you so long, and yet you have not known Me, Philip? He who has seen Me has seen the Father; so how can you say, 'Show us the Father'?"*

Jesus was letting His disciples know that all the wonders, miracles, kindness, and goodness they has seen displayed was who the Father was. This was earth-shaking for them. A completely different view of God was beginning to form in their minds and hearts. The same thing must happen to us as well. Most of us live in a very performance-oriented society and culture. Perhaps we have grown up where performance was rewarded or even love was withheld if we didn't measure up. This creates in us an unspoken mentality that "If I perform well, I am loved. However, if I don't perform well, I am rejected and even unloved." This imbeds in us a wrong perspective of God. This is even reinforced in religious circles. Fear and guilt are used to control the masses. It's not that we shouldn't perform well. It is, however, the motivation behind the desire that is critical. If I am performing so I will be accepted, this is a trap. However, if I am performing because I long to please the one I love, this is correct. In other words, according to First John 4:18-19 our reason behind our desire to please is the love we have already received. We are not seeking to be loved as a result of our performance.

> *There is no fear in love; but perfect love casts out fear, because fear involves torment. But he who fears has not been made perfect in love. We love Him because He first loved us.*

What a statement. There is no fear in love! Real love does not have fear associated with it. Real love is a result of having been loved. So when we experience the total and complete acceptance of the Father and His love, it births the ability to love Him back. This causes us to perform.

This is why Jesus said if we loved Him, we would obey Him. John 14:23 states the connection between love and obeying the Lord.

> *Jesus answered and said to him, "If anyone loves Me, he will keep My word; and My Father will love him, and We will come to him and make Our home with him."*

When we experience the love of the Father, we are empowered to love Him, which grants us the strength to obey Him. The point being that our revelation of God as Father is critical to us serving Him acceptably. This would seem to have been one of the main objectives as Jesus taught the masses and His disciples. He wanted them to get how good God is as our Father. This is critical to prayer. We will never go any deeper in prayer than our revelation of God as our Father allows! This is why Jesus spent so much time seeking to convince them of the Father and His goodness. For instance, the story of the prodigal son is a revelation of the Father's goodness. Luke

15:20-32 shows the father in this story and his acceptance of the son who left and his pleading with the one who stayed home.

> *And he arose and came to his father. But when he was still a great way off, his father saw him and had compassion, and ran and fell on his neck and kissed him. And the son said to him, "Father, I have sinned against heaven and in your sight, and am no longer worthy to be called your son."*
>
> *But the father said to his servants, "Bring out the best robe and put it on him, and put a ring on his hand and sandals on his feet. And bring the fatted calf here and kill it, and let us eat and be merry; for this my son was dead and is alive again; he was lost and is found." And they began to be merry.*
>
> *Now his older son was in the field. And as he came and drew near to the house, he heard music and dancing. So he called one of the servants and asked what these things meant. And he said to him, "Your brother has come, and because he has received him safe and sound, your father has killed the fatted calf."*
>
> *But he was angry and would not go in. Therefore his father came out and pleaded with him. So he answered and said to his father, "Lo, these many years I have been serving you; I never transgressed your commandment at any time; and yet you never gave me a young goat, that I might make merry with my friends. But as soon as this son of yours came, who has devoured your livelihood with harlots, you killed the fatted calf for him."*
>
> *And he said to him, "Son, you are always with me, and all that I have is yours. It was right that we should make*

merry and be glad, for your brother was dead and is alive again, and was lost and is found."

The son we normally call the prodigal took the stuff of his father and wasted it with harlots and very sinful living. When he decides to go home, he doesn't expect his father to have a heart toward him. He thinks he's going to have to beg just to be as one of the hired servants. To his dismay and pleasure the father throws his arms around him, loves him, restores him, and has a party in his honor. Wow! This must have amazed the son to the point of it seeming too good to be true.

Please notice that the goodness and generosity of the father weren't received by the older brother. Even though he stayed at home while his younger brother did what he did, the older brother is bitter, angry, and disgusted with the whole party atmosphere. He feels the younger brother should be made to pay for his transgressions and not be forgiven this easily. Plus, the older brother feels mistreated and unappreciated. All this is happening because he doesn't understand the goodness of his father. Neither boy has the revelation of how good their father is. The younger son's lack of understanding his father's goodness is seen in his expectation of having to beg to just be a servant. The older brother's lack of understanding of the goodness of his father is seen in his attitude toward the younger son and the father having to explain that everything belongs to him.

In Jewish culture, the firstborn was to receive a double portion of the inheritance. The older son, not knowing the goodness of the father, couldn't see the future that awaited him. Both boys had a lack of realizing how good their father was. So do we. I am convinced that we underestimate the goodness of our heavenly Father. In fact, only by revelation can we begin to get an awareness of His generosity and kindness. Jesus told stories and parables to try and get us to see it.

He sought to help us understand that our view of the goodness of God releases us into new spheres of grace. Likewise, the lack thereof could have devastating impact on us. For instance, in the parable of the talents the man with the one talent entrusted into his care had a view of the master that was harsh and uncaring. Matthew 25:24-30 gives insight into the psyche of the one who was deemed unfaithful by the master.

> *Then he who had received the one talent came and said, "Lord, I knew you to be a hard man, reaping where you have not sown, and gathering where you have not scattered seed. And I was afraid, and went and hid your talent in the ground. Look, there you have what is yours."*
>
> *But his lord answered and said to him, "You wicked and lazy servant, you knew that I reap where I have not sown, and gather where I have not scattered seed. So you ought to have deposited my money with the bankers, and at my coming I would have received back my own with interest. So take the talent from him, and give it to him who has ten talents.*
>
> *"For to everyone who has, more will be given, and he will have abundance; but from him who does not have, even what he has will be taken away. And cast the unprofitable servant into the outer darkness. There will be weeping and gnashing of teeth."*

Notice that the servant claimed it was his fear that drove him to do nothing with what had been entrusted to him. We can tend to think that our fear justifies faithlessness. Yet the master said he was a lazy and wicked servant. We must recognize how the Lord sees our unbelief. Hebrews 3:12 cautions us to not allow a heart of unbelief to develop in us.

Beware, brethren, lest there be in any of you an evil heart
of unbelief in departing from the living God.

Unbelief is seen as an evil thing before the Lord. It is not seen as part of our humanity that is to be pitied. It is seen as that which is against God and needs to be repented of. Revelation 21:8 list those who are fearful with all sorts of wicked activities.

But the cowardly, unbelieving, abominable, murderers,
sexually immoral, sorcerers, idolaters, and all liars shall
have their part in the lake which burns with fire and
brimstone, which is the second death.

Wow! Cowards are listed with murders, fornicators, adulterers, idolaters, those practicing witchcraft, and others involved in all sorts of wickedness. These will find themselves in the lake burning with fire and brimstone. This tells us we cannot afford these *lesser* sins. We must cast off the cowardice, fearfulness, and unbelief that would cling to us. We mustn't allow it place in our life. When we look at the man who did nothing with his one talent trusted to him, it was because of his perspective he had of the master and lord. He said he knew him to be a hard man with expectations of those he trusted his valuables with. This was his excuse for why he did nothing with what had been given him.

He was *afraid* to lose it. His *fear* had its roots in the way he saw the master. The way we see God has everything to do with the way we function. If we see Him as a loving, caring God who encourages us to step out in faith, then we are emboldened to do so. On the other hand, if we see Him as hard, austere, and having unreal expectations, this can paralyze us with inactivity and unbelief. The interesting thing about this story is the master gave the one with one talent no wiggle room. His response was that his perspective of who he was should have been motivation. If he really believed him to be hard and with unreal expectations, this should have pressed him, even in his fear, to act. The man was judged based on his perspective of who the master was. Right or wrong, his perspective determined his judgment. The psalmist backs up this idea in Psalm 18:24-27.

> *Therefore the Lord has recompensed me according to my*
> *righteousness,*
>
> *According to the cleanness of my hands in His sight.*
>
> *With the merciful You will show Yourself merciful;*
>
> *With a blameless man You will show Yourself blameless;*
>
> *With the pure You will show Yourself pure;*
>
> *And with the devious You will show Yourself shrewd.*
>
> *For You will save the humble people,*
>
> *But will bring down haughty looks.*

Whatever revelation we have of the Lord, that will be the realm from which we are judged. The problem is that ideas about the Lord that are not completely correct can neutralize us and destroy faith in us. However, the Lord doesn't allow this to be an excuse. It seems that His perspective is that regardless of who we see Him to be, it should motivate us to faith and good works. However, when we understand the graciousness of who He is, it moves us to real faith and right activities.

Another place where we see this is the parable of the vineyard where different groups went to work in a landowner's vineyard. The first group went to work on the basis of agreement. In other words, they had a contract with the landowner that said they would get this much money for this much work. Every other group after the first one went on the basis of *whatever is right*. In other words, they had no agreement, just a confidence in the goodness, generosity, and liberality of the landowner to do what was right. We see this in Matthew 20:1-7.

> *For the kingdom of heaven is like a landowner who went out early in the morning to hire laborers for his vineyard. Now when he had agreed with the laborers for a denarius a day, he sent them into his vineyard. And he went out about the third hour and saw others standing idle in the marketplace, and said to them, "You also go into the vineyard, and whatever is right I will give you." So they went. Again he went out about the sixth and the ninth hour, and did likewise. And about the eleventh hour he went out and found others standing idle, and said to them, "Why have you been standing here idle all day?" They said to him, "Because no one hired us." He said to them, "You also go into the vineyard, and whatever is right you will receive."*

When you stop and think about this practically, what person would agree to work on a job without knowing what they will get paid? Only those who are convinced of the generosity and kindness of the employer, business owner, or in this case the owner of the vineyard. The first group that agreed speaks of the Jews whom Jesus came to first. They were bound by law and could not see past Moses. However, Jesus was sent to them first. The protocol of heaven demanded they be given the first opportunity to receive the message of the kingdom of God. Matthew 15:23-24 sees Jesus initially refusing to heal the daughter of a Gentile woman. This was because Jesus was sent to the Jews first.

> *But He answered her not a word.*

And His disciples came and urged Him, saying, "Send her away, for she cries out after us."

But He answered and said, "I was not sent except to the lost sheep of the house of Israel."

Jesus' refusal to heal this woman's daughter was because the house of Israel had to be given the right of first refusal. When the Jews rejected the Messiah and His message, it could then go to the Gentiles. This is also why Jesus instructed those He sent out in Matthew 10:5-8 to only go to the house of Israel.

These twelve Jesus sent out and commanded them, saying: "Do not go into the way of the Gentiles, and do not enter a city of the Samaritans. But go rather to the lost sheep of the house of Israel. And as you go, preach, saying, 'The kingdom of heaven is at hand.' Heal the sick, cleanse the lepers, raise the dead, cast out demons. Freely you have received, freely give."

Israel had to see a demonstration of the kingdom of God. Once this was done, God could righteously and legally go to the Gentiles. We see this happening in the days of Paul. When the Jews he was ministering to rejected and persecuted the gospel of the kingdom, Paul turned to the Gentiles. Acts 13:45-46 shows Paul boldly making a pronouncement that they were now going to the Gentiles with the gospel.

But when the Jews saw the multitudes, they were filled with envy; and contradicting and blaspheming, they opposed the things spoken by Paul. Then Paul and Barnabas grew bold and said, "It was necessary that the word of God should be spoken to you first; but since you reject it, and judge yourselves unworthy of everlasting life, behold, we turn to the Gentiles."

This statement by Paul epitomized the intent of God. When the Jews rejected the goodness of God in favor of the law and its legalism, this was what God needed to send His word to the Gentiles. This is what Jesus is teaching in the parable of the vineyard. The first group, the Jews, would *agree* or have a contract with the landowner. All the other groups, which speak of the Gentile nations, would serve on the basis of grace or whatever is right. They would have a revelation of the goodness, kindness, and liberality of the Lord. The result was they would get exponential blessings and multiplication because of the basis they served from. The Jews would be provoked to jealousy because of the goodness of God to the Gentiles. We see this in Matthew 20:10-12.

> *But when the first came, they supposed that they would receive more; and they likewise received each a denarius. And when they had received it, they complained against the landowner, saying, "These last men have worked only one hour, and you made them equal to us who have borne the burden and the heat of the day."*

Those who had agreed with the landowner supposed they would have received more because of what the ones who had labored less had gotten. However, they got what they had agreed to. Paul would later declare that God would use the Gentiles to provoke the Jews to jealousy. This is what Jesus is prophesying will happen through this parable. The Jews' rejection of what was offered to them would allow the Gentiles entrance. This would cause the Jews to come to jealousy. Romans 10:19 tells us that God would use people who were not a people to stir Israel.

> *But I say, did Israel not know? First Moses says: "I will provoke you to jealousy by those who are not a nation, I will move you to anger by a foolish nation."*

God's goodness shown to the Gentiles is designed to stir Israel to want God again. This is one of the things Jesus is revealing in this parable. He is showing those bound in agreement to God will become even angered by the kindness of God to another nation. They will begin to get another idea of who God is. Paul addresses this again in Romans 11:11 when he clearly states the fall of the Jewish people will result in the Gentiles receiving mercy from the Lord.

> *I say then, have they stumbled that they should fall? Certainly not! But through their fall, to provoke them to jealousy, salvation has come to the Gentiles.*

God desires to show His kindness in unprecedented ways in these times. As much as the parable of the vineyard is about the Jews, their legalism, and their unwillingness to transition into the New Covenant, and the Gentiles and their receiving of grace, it's also about any of us who are bound with legalism and a wrong perspective of God. Those who *agreed* with the landowner had limitations on them. Those who trusted His kindness received exponential multiplication as they served in the vineyard. The principle is that we must transition from a legalistic view of who God is to one that will see His graciousness. This is critical to us receiving the fullness of Him into our life. The Bible says that Abraham found this out about God. Romans 4:1-4 gives us insight into what Abraham found on his journey.

> *What then shall we say that Abraham our father has found according to the flesh? For if Abraham was justified by works, he has something to boast about, but not before God. For what does the Scripture say? "Abraham*

*believed God, and it was accounted to him for righteous-
ness." Now to him who works, the wages are not counted
as grace but as debt.*

I love the way Scripture puts this here. Abraham found some
things out as he functioned in the flesh. In other words, he discovered some things on his journey with God. Just like us, we have
different perspectives at the end of our journey with God than we
probably did in the beginning. What we might be so certain of when
we start, becomes adjusted on the way. For instance, I really like what
I heard years ago about Moses and his rod. We all know that Moses'
encounter with God at the burning bush transformed him and his
rod into that which would deliver Israel from Egypt (see Exod. 4:1-9).
But where did this rod that Moses carried come from? Most likely he
found it on his journey. I'm sure there wasn't a *rod store* somewhere
where he purchased it. He *picked it up* somewhere as he went. It was
just a normal, natural stick. Yet when through the encounter with
God the power of God came into and upon this stick, it was used to
perform signs and wonders in Egypt. With this rod Moses delivered
Israel from its Egyptian bondage and slavery.

We each *pick things up* on our journey. They may seem like
insignificant ideas, principles, and even revelations at the moment.
However, when the power of God touches that which we picked
up on our journey, it can be life-changing. We are now carrying
something of power and might to bring deliverance to people from
the Lord.

When I read of Abraham having *found* some things in the flesh,
this is what I think of. As Abraham journeyed, he discovered revelations of who God is and how He operates. Abraham was an Old
Testament man with New Testament revelation. This is what made
him so powerful in his generation. Through the revelation he had

found in and about God, he radically changed his times and shaped the future. The verses in Romans give us insight into the revelation Abraham picked up on his journey. He discovered that God doesn't respond to works or performance but rather faith. We don't impress God with works of righteousness but rather faith in His graciousness and goodness. Paul said if it was of works, it was of debt. In other words, we say our prayers, read our Bible, go to services, pay our tithes and other activities—therefore, God *owes us or is indebted to us.*

One illustration of this is when we go to work during the week our labors make our employer our debtor. Therefore, we expect a paycheck at the end of the work period. We don't consider it charity because our employer owes us this because of our energy, time, skill, education, and efforts. My employer is, in essence, my debtor because of my work. Abraham discovered this is not the basis God operates from. We don't work to make Him our debtor. Instead, we move in faith in His graciousness, kindness, and goodness. This may not change one thing I do. I still pray, read the Word, go to service, pay tithes, and other activities. The difference is why I am doing it and where I am doing it from in the spirit realm. I am not working to make God my debtor, but instead I love Him because of His goodness and kindness. This is what Abraham found out. This is the transition we also must make. We do not want to agree in a legalistic way with the Lord, but from revelation discover His goodness as our loving Father. Once this happens, we are ready to approach God as Father as Jesus taught us.

The next thing that must occur is the Spirit of adoption must be received. It is the Spirit of adoption or the Holy Spirit who reveals the nature of God as our Father. Romans 8:14-17 tells us the necessity of this ongoing encounter.

For as many as are led by the Spirit of God, these are sons of God. For you did not receive the spirit of bondage again to fear, but you received the Spirit of adoption by whom we cry out, "Abba, Father." The Spirit Himself bears witness with our spirit that we are children of God, and if children, then heirs—heirs of God and joint heirs with Christ, if indeed we suffer with Him, that we may also be glorified together.

This whole verse of Scripture is describing coming out from under the law and into the liberty of the Spirit of God. Being freed from the spirit of bondage again to fear is talking about the law and legalism and the shame and condemnation it produces. Remember that the law makes sin exceedingly sinful. Romans 7:13 echoes this truth.

Has then what is good become death to me? Certainly not! But sin, that it might appear sin, was producing death in me through what is good, so that sin through the commandment might become exceedingly sinful.

When sin becomes exceedingly sinful through the commandment or the law, it produces shame or death in me. Jesus' work on my behalf on the cross answers the demands of the law. Therefore, I am not brought back into bondage to fear and filled with shame. I am instead positioned to receive the Spirit of adoption that reveals the goodness and kindness of the Father toward me. We have been set free to walk under the constraints of the Spirit of God.

The Spirit of adoption causes us to cry out, "Abba, Father." In other words, we have a revelation of God as our Father that produces an empowerment to pray. To fully understand this, we must first realize that the Spirit of adoption is the Holy Spirit. One of the main functions of the Holy Spirit is to empower us to pray from the unction He provides. Romans 8:26-27 shows this attribute of the Holy Spirit at work.

> *Likewise the Spirit also helps in our weaknesses. For we do not know what we should pray for as we ought, but the Spirit Himself makes intercession for us with groanings which cannot be uttered. Now He who searches the hearts knows what the mind of the Spirit is, because He makes intercession for the saints according to the will of God.*

This scripture declares we are weak when it comes to the realm of prayer. The Holy Spirit helps in these places of weakness and feebleness. In the natural we have no power to be effective in prayer. Prayer requires the supernatural strength of the Spirit of God. Notice that without the Holy Spirit we don't know what we are to pray for. It would seem simple enough to decide what we are to pray for. We can see needs, desires, and necessities and should be able to figure it out. However, the reason it speaks of helping us discern *what* to pray for is because prayer is not just making requests but actually moving things in the spirit realm so answers can manifest. There are times we need the discernment, unction, and inspiration of the Holy Spirit to pray effectively. It may not be a matter of what seems apparent, but literally something behind the scenes in the spirit realm needs to be addressed. In these places, we need the power of the Holy Spirit to grant us understanding, wisdom, and discernment to pray.

The verses we cited also say the Holy Spirit prays for us according to the will of God. In other words, sometimes through groanings, tears, and even the prayer language of tongues the Holy Spirit makes intercession for us. We may not even know what we are touching. However, the Spirit through us is praying in accordance with the passion and even intercession of Jesus Himself. Remember that Jesus ever lives to intercede. Hebrews 7:25 gives us this wonderful truth.

> *Therefore He is also able to save to the uttermost those who come to God through Him, since He always lives to make intercession for them.*

Not only did Jesus die on the cross, was buried, then resurrected and ascended, He is now praying. Jesus is interceding to pray us into the reality of everything He died for us to have. This is what being *saved to the uttermost* implies. Jesus ever lives to intercede for the purposes of God to be fulfilled through us. When the Holy Spirit makes intercession in us, through us, and for us, I believe it is in agreement with what Jesus is interceding. Through the ministry of the Holy Spirit, we begin to attach ourselves to Jesus' present-day prayer ministry. We join ourselves in the spirit realm as His Body to His headship. Remember that He is the Head and we are the Body of Christ. Whatever He is doing as the Head we are to agree with as the body. First John 4:17 helps us realize that whatever Jesus is presently doing, we as His Body should be doing the same.

> *Love has been perfected among us in this: that we may have boldness in the day of judgment; because as He is, so are we in this world.*

Notice that whatever He is, we are. We are tied to Him as our natural bodies are tied to our physical heads. The result is our heads tell our bodies what to do. It is the same in the spirit world with Jesus and His church. Whatever He is doing, we are connected to. If He is the intercessor, then it would stand to reason that we partake of that intercession. This is why the Holy Spirit makes intercession through us. He pours the passion of Jesus' intercession through us. Please be aware that our present-tense joining to Jesus is what grants us boldness in the day of judgment. As we live out our lives in union with Jesus and His intercession, the day of judgment will hold no trepidation for us. There will be great boldness and confidence, because we have spent our lives fulfilling the passion of our Head in the earth!

When the Spirit of adoption creates the cry of "Abba Father" in our hearts, it is because the revelation of who God is as our Father becomes real. God is no longer far-off and distant God incapable of intimacy. He becomes a very real and present God who is our Father. Part of this process is the healing of wounds generated from improper and insufficient fathering. All of us have been subjected to this on some level. There are no perfect fathers except one. He is our heavenly Father. Hebrews 12:9-10 says our fathers disciplined us according to their own judgment and will.

> *Furthermore, we have had human fathers who corrected us, and we paid them respect. Shall we not much more readily be in subjection to the Father of spirits and live? For they indeed for a few days chastened us as seemed best to them, but He for our profit, that we may be partakers of His holiness.*

Our natural fathers from a limited perspective sought to influence us and instruct us. They did what seemed best to them. As a result of them being human and filled with fallacy, their judgment at times and at best was suspect. Plus our fathers carried the wounds of their own lives and the way they were fathered. The result was imperfect and insufficient fathering. Many people because of this carry wounds and fears from the way they were fathered. The Spirit of adoption comes to heal those wounds, fears, and traumas so we can see who our heavenly Father is. I believe this is what one of God's intents was in requiring Abraham to get away from his father's house. Genesis 12:1-3 tells of God revealing Himself to Abraham and asking him to leave everything to possess a land and birth a nation and nations as a father.

Now the Lord had said to Abram:

"Get out of your country,

From your family

And from your father's house,

To a land that I will show you.

I will make you a great nation;

I will bless you

And make your name great;

And you shall be a blessing.

I will bless those who bless you,

And I will curse him who curses you;

And in you all the families of the earth shall be blessed."

Abram in the Hebrew means *high father.* The name *Abraham* that God would change it to in Genesis 17:5 means *a father of a multitude.*

No longer shall your name be called Abram, but your name shall be Abraham; for I have made you a father of many nations.

It seems that it was always understood that Abraham was to be a significant father. Even before God changed his name, Abram's name implied the fathering effect he was to have. When God changed his name, He simply added to Abram's name *ah* which was a portion of God's name as Jehov*ah*. After years of Abram's walk with God, the influence of his natural father, Terah, had been replaced with the influence of God. Abraham now carried the nature of the heavenly Father. This occurred by God removing Abraham from his father's house. If Abraham was to father nations into their destiny, he had to have the nature of God his Father. He had to potentially be healed of any wounds and fears associated with his natural father's house. Every wrong concept of fathering had to be removed and replaced in Abraham. This was a part of the decades of shaping that God was doing in Abraham on his journey.

We too must go through a similar process. The Spirit of adoption must be allowed to work out of us the contamination of insufficient fathering and put into us the nature of the heavenly Father. Jesus spoke of us being the children of our heavenly Father. Matthew 5:44-45 shows Jesus challenging the disciples to be the children of their Father in heaven.

> *But I say to you, love your enemies, bless those who curse you, do good to those who hate you, and pray for those who spitefully use you and persecute you, that you may be sons of your Father in heaven; for He makes His sun rise on the evil and on the good, and sends rain on the just and on the unjust.*

Jesus is declaring that God is a loving heavenly Father who even loves those who have no heart for Him. Jesus is doing two things through this statement about the Father. He is revealing the goodness and kindness of the Father but also pressing the disciples to reflect this same nature as His sons. When we are fathered by the heavenly Father through the Spirit of adoption, the very nature of the Father is formed in us. This is because the need to be abusing, neglecting, abandoning, and selfish has been removed by the love of our perfect heavenly Father. It is replaced with His care and heart even toward those who have no heart for Him or us. We are free to love from His passion and love unconditionally.

The first time I began to get a picture of this was in my mid-twenties. I was at a men's retreat where a minister was speaking on the Father heart of God. My natural father was a very good man. He had his faults, as we all do, yet he never did me damage in a significant way as my dad. I wasn't carrying around a lot of baggage from my growing-up years. On the other hand, a minister friend also in the meeting had a history with his dad that was very uncaring, abusive, and neglectful. As the ministry happened that night, my friend became undone. I had never seen this man so broken and emotional. As they ministered to him, two other men had to hold him up as the travail he was in was so heavy and intense. He did more than weep. The emotion pouring through him was so intense that it would have made others uncomfortable. It was the Spirit of adoption healing the wounds and scars of improper fathering this man had carried through his childhood and into adulthood. He later told me during the process the Holy Spirit whispered to him, "Just cooperate with Me." In other words, the Holy Spirit was saying, "Let me in this moment heal the wounds, hurts, and scars inflicted by the rejection of your natural father. Open your emotions and heart with full access and surrender to My touch. Don't close down in fear and shame in this moment. Grant Me full availability right now, and I will heal the years of the refusal of your natural father." My friend was changed in that moment. A revelation of the Father heart of God toward him was found.

All that he had ever been looking for concerning love and acceptance came to him that night. He was forever changed that day. In varying degrees this must happen to all of us. Perhaps it will not be that level of emotional intensity, but it will be deep and meaningful as the love of the Father washes away any rejection and pain of neglect and abandonment. The Spirit of adoption unveils Abba Father to us.

I too have had my own encounters with the Spirit of adoption and Abba Father. For many, this will occur during times of failure. It will be when you feel that there is no way God can love you. You are afraid that you have messed up so bad that there is no way God would have anything to do with you. The truth is when we are living life *successfully,* when we are on top of things, we feel good about ourselves, the revelation of God as Abba Father from the Spirit of adoption is not readily received. We have no perceived need that is crying out. However, when we are disgusted with ourselves, when we detest who we are and what we have done, in these times we need the acceptance of the Father. It seems these times are the place where God comes through His Holy Spirit and shows His unconditional, never-changing love for us.

Just such a thing happened to me. I had compromised my walk with the Lord. No, I hadn't stolen something or cheated anyone or committed adultery or any other grievous sins we might think about. However, I had failed and was in complete condemnation and feared that God was done with me. I felt altogether unworthy and was confident that God would be justified in rejecting me and any purpose of His associated with me. In the midst of this I went into prayer to plead with Him concerning this thing. I would pray as David prayed in Psalm 51:10-11 when he had committed adultery with Bathsheba.

Create in me a clean heart, O God,

And renew a steadfast spirit within me.

Do not cast me away from Your presence,

And do not take Your Holy Spirit from me.

Suddenly as I was praying and seeking His face in the midst of my failure, shame, and guilt, I felt what I can only describe as God's covenant love settle on me. It was the love of the Father coming to assure me that in this place of failure His love for me was steadfast and amazing. I knew at that moment that my destiny wasn't lost. In this instant, I became aware that God was my Father and would never leave me nor forsake me.

This was a pivotal time for me. I had grown up in a very performance-oriented environment. I knew I was loved but also knew performance was very important. I didn't perform in this setting because I didn't want to disappoint; I performed out of fear. I suddenly understood that my obedience was to flow not just from a fear of the Lord, but also out of a love for God born from the love of the Father for me. I knew God loved me in the midst of my failure, not just when I did well. This changed everything. I have been on this journey of discovering the Father's love for me now for three-plus decades. This is not something we are supposed to know just theologically but also through experience. Romans 5:5 tells us there is a hope we have that makes us not ashamed. In other words, it deals with any shame and guilt we carry.

> *Now hope does not disappoint, because the love of God*
> *has been poured out in our hearts by the Holy Spirit who*
> *was given to us.*

There is a connection between the love of God poured into our hearts and the hope it births in us. When we know how much God loves us, every sense of hopelessness concerning the future is removed. The love God revealed in our hearts gives us the awareness that we have a futu e. It's a good future with good things planned for us. This stirs faith in us all because of the Holy Spirit, or the Spirit of adoption pouring God's love into our hearts. Jesus referred to this idea of God's mercy and forgiveness revealing His love and the impact it has on us.

Jesus was invited to a Pharisee's house for a meal. A woman who was a sinner came in and begins to wash His feet with her tears. This was appalling to the religious. They even said in their hearts that if Jesus were a real prophet, He would have known what kind of woman this was. Jesus perceiving the thoughts spoke a quick story of two debtors in Luke 7:40-47.

> *And Jesus answered and said to him, "Simon, I have something to say to you."*
>
> *So he said, "Teacher, say it."*
>
> *"There was a certain creditor who had two debtors. One owed five hundred denarii, and the other fifty. And when they had nothing with which to repay, he freely forgave them both. Tell Me, therefore, which of them will love him more?"*
>
> *Simon answered and said, "I suppose the one whom he forgave more."*
>
> *And He said to him, "You have rightly judged." Then He turned to the woman and said to Simon, "Do you see this woman? I entered your house; you gave Me no water for My feet, but she has washed My feet with her tears and wiped them with the hair of her head. You gave Me no kiss, but this woman has not ceased to kiss My feet since the time I came in. You did not anoint My head with oil, but this woman has anointed My feet with fragrant oil. Therefore I say to you, her sins, which are many, are forgiven, for she loved much. But to whom little is forgiven, the same loves little."*

When there is a great awareness of our sin, when it is forgiven, it births in us a great love. The problem with this Pharisee was he was just as sinful as the woman; he just didn't recognize it. There was a self-righteousness that these religious people were walking in. This self-righteousness didn't allow them to see their own desperate need. The thing this woman had that they didn't, was a revelation of her need to be forgiven. The more we see our need for a Savior, the more we value, appreciate, and love Him when He shows up. This is why David spoke of the blessedness of being forgiven in Psalm 32:1.

Blessed is he whose transgression is forgiven,

Whose sin is covered.

When we are forgiven, the joy of being freed excites our soul. Forgiveness received gives us back our future and our hope. The one who is forgiven also greatly loves. I have watched in the church through the years when people get radically saved and born again. Their love for Jesus is great. One of the reasons for this is because they are experiencing the joy of forgiveness. There is nothing like it. This is why First John 2:12-13 among other things speaks to us as little children and the excitement of being forgiven.

I write to you, little children,

Because your sins are forgiven you for His name's sake.

I write to you, fathers,

Because you have known Him who is from the beginning.

I write to you, young men,

Because you have overcome the wicked one.

I write to you, little children,

Because you have known the Father.

In these two verses, *little children* is spoken of twice. It is the Greek word *paidon* and it means a childling and an infant. It is speaking of a very young believer who has recently been converted. Notice two things they *know*. They know they are forgiven and they know they have a Father. These two things go together. A revelation of God as Father and of His forgiveness gives us the right view of Him. It speaks to us of the Father's love and how much He cares for us. All of this is connected to the revelation of God as our good Father. This is the job of the Spirit of adoption to create this in us.

It is quite interesting to me that the Spirit of adoption creates the cry of *Abba Father* in our hearts (see Rom. 8:15). Paul was not being redundant when he spoke of *Abba Father*. He wasn't just trying to figure out a different way to say the same thing. He was actually revealing two different aspect of God as our Father. *Abba* in Strong's Concordance is a *father as vocative. Vocative* is a cry to someone or something. So when the term *Abba* is used, it is referring to a familiarity with God as Abba that would allow us to call upon Him. It is an endearing term of intimacy and familiarity with God. He is my *Abba*.

Father, on the other hand, is a term of authority. A father in a home isn't supposed to just create love and security. He is also one who protects, creates boundaries, and brings order to the home by the authority he carries. Whereas *Abba* is about intimacy and closeness, *Father* is about authority and order. Father is a term of authority. This is very necessary. If all we had was Abba there would be no order. However, if all we had was Father there could be no real affection and love. Both aspects are necessary. In fact, the emphasis of one aspect without an awareness of the other has caused many believers to be unbalanced in their view of God as Father.

It is imperative that we see this if we are going to approach God as Father and step into the dimensions it opens for us. If all we know of God in His Fatherhood is Abba, it can tend toward lawlessness. This in my estimation is presently what is occurring in the church with the heavy emphasis on grace without emphasis on holiness and purity to balance it out. Please do not misconstrue what I am saying. I am a product of grace. I can say as Paul, I am what I am by the grace of God (see I Cor. 15:10). Having said this, I am an advocate for the right grace message to be preached. Not the one that says there is no need for repentance. Not the one that says all our sins are forgiven past, present, and future without any need for our acknowledgement of them on any level. Not the one that says you can live however you want and it's okay with God. Not the one that says there are portions of Scripture no longer relevant to our contemporary world. I say no! I want the right grace message preached. For instance, let's preach the one from Titus 2:11-14.

> *For the grace of God that brings salvation has appeared to all men, teaching us that, denying ungodliness and worldly lusts, we should live soberly, righteously, and godly in the present age, looking for the blessed hope and glorious appearing of our great God and Savior Jesus Christ, who gave Himself for us, that He might redeem us from every lawless deed and purify for Himself His own special people, zealous for good works.*

The real grace of God that brings real salvation teaches us to live holy. It causes us to look for our reward in that which is coming and not just the here and now. It makes us have a passion to be His people, zealous and passionate for good works. Having said this, we must be careful not to turn the grace of God into what Jude spoke of in Jude 4.

For certain men have crept in unnoticed, who long ago were marked out for this condemnation, ungodly men, who turn the grace of our God into lewdness and deny the only Lord God and our Lord Jesus Christ.

They use the grace of God as a license to sin and to promote it. These must be forsaken. This is what occurs if we only know the Abba side of God's Fatherhood. However, if all we know is the authoritarian side of God as Father, we can become legalists. We all know "fathers" who rule their families with a fist of iron. They expect complete submission of their wives and their children. They create an atmosphere of fear that controls everyone in it. This is not the Fatherhood of God. He is, however, our Father. He is in authority. As God who is our Father, He will discipline us for our own good and so we can be partakers of His holiness. This is uncovered in Hebrews 12:5-10.

And you have forgotten the exhortation which speaks to you as to sons:

"My son, do not despise the chastening of the Lord,

Nor be discouraged when you are rebuked by Him;

For whom the Lord loves He chastens,

And scourges every son whom He receives."

If you endure chastening, God deals with you as with sons; for what son is there whom a father does not chasten? But if you are without chastening, of which all have become partakers, then you are illegitimate and not sons. Furthermore, we have had human fathers who corrected us, and we paid them respect. Shall we not much more readily be in subjection to the Father of spirits and live? For they indeed for a few days chastened us as seemed best

to them, but He for our profit, that we may be partakers
of His holiness.

These verses are very clear. We have a Father who will discipline us so we can grow into holiness and be like Him. This scripture unveils several critical truths about God as the Father who loves us enough to chasten us. First of all, God's chastening is a sure sign of His love for us.

His chastening hand is a demonstration that He has an awesome plan for us and desires us to qualify for it. Second, His discipline of us says that we are really His. He only disciplines those who belong to Him. If we are not experiencing His discipline, then we are *not His*. Third, the discipline is so we can be partakers of His holiness. He desires us to be holy as He is holy. First Peter 1:14-16 tells us that God passionately desires a holy people set apart to Him.

As obedient children, not conforming yourselves to the
former lusts, as in your ignorance; but as He who called
you is holy, you also be holy in all your conduct, because
it is written, "Be holy, for I am holy."

We are not to allow our own lusts and desires to rule us. Through the empowerment of the Spirit and the chastening of the hand of the Lord we become holy as He is holy. Being holy is not first and foremost about activities. Holiness is to be uncommon and set a part from that which is common. It is to be a different people from all other peoples. Anybody can follow the lust of their flesh. It takes one disciplined by the Lord to grow in holiness and allow His nature to manifest through them. I have found that the Holy Spirit in me will press me to realms of holiness. He creates within me a desire, longing, and cry to be holy as He is holy. A big part of this process is the disciplining hand of the Father. Every son that He loves, He disciplines.

To have a proper perspective of the Father's discipline of us we should also recognize what the terms *chastening* and *rebuke* actually mean. These are not the activities of an angry God. They are the efforts of our loving Father to mature us into His likeness. The word *chastening* in the Greek is *paideia*. It means to educate or train. It means disciplinarian correcting and to nurture and instruct. It doesn't mean God is going to cause something bad and evil to happen to you. He is not into punishment, but rather discipline. Punishment is retributive. Discipline is about training us for our future. If you were disciplined in anger by your parents, it's probably hard for you to equate this. However, God as our Father is not about making us *pay for our wrongs.* He is seeking through discipline to instruct us and alter our behavior to align with His heart.

The word *rebuke* in the Greek is *elegcho*. It means to admonish, convict, and tell a fault. Neither of these words have anything to do with evil happening to us. They are about the conviction of the Holy Spirit speaking to us and causing us to recognize our wrong attitudes, behaviors, words, and actions. It is the Lord allowing us to realize places in our lives that do not reflect Him or line up with His desires. I have also seen the loving kindness of God in Him correcting us so evil will not come to us. Peter speaks of suffering because of our own activities. First Peter 4:15 tells us to not suffer because of our own foolish activities.

> *But let none of you suffer as a murderer, a thief, an evildoer, or as a busybody in other people's matters.*

In other words, it is possible for us to go into hard places because we have lived in unwise ways. I have literally watched the Lord come with words of correction to seek to stop this from happening. If we choose to listen, we can escape major consequences in the future. If we ignore the words of correction, we will have to walk through places God never intended. May the Lord grant us always an ear to hear what He is saying to us from His love and kindness.

One more thing that is helpful to be aware of is our response when we are corrected. Habakkuk spoke of this in Habakkuk 2:1.

> *I will stand my watch*
> *And set myself on the rampart,*
> *And watch to see what He will say to me,*
> *And what I will answer when I am corrected.*

The prophet seems to have a watch on his heart to make sure he gives the right response when God corrects him. Our response is very important to the correcting hand of God. It can determine what kind of future we have. Again, the writer of Hebrews admonishes us in the scripture we read of two extremes we can fall into when corrected by the Lord. He says we shouldn't despise or be discouraged when corrected. The word *despise* in the Greek is *oligoreo* and it means to have little regard for, to disesteem. In other words, when God comes with His correcting words or conviction, we don't pay attention to them. We disregard them and treat them lightly. If we do this, we will live to regret not paying attention to His cautions and corrections. We must guard against responding so lightly.

The other word *discouraged* is the Greek word *ekluo*. It means to faint or to cause to dissolve. This means that we get under the word of correction. In other words, the word of discipline causes us to want to give up and quit. This is because we don't understand the motivation of God in it. These are the two extremes in responding to God's correction as our Father. One is we treat it lightly and dismiss it while the other is we fall under condemnation and guilt and want to quit. Neither of these responses are right. We must embrace and order our steps in the fear of the Lord when we are corrected. When we do, it works in us the holiness of the Lord that secures a good future for us because we have paid attention to the chastening hand of God. This is how Jesus lived in His earthly life. Luke 2:43 refers to Jesus as the *Boy Jesus*.

> *When they had finished the days, as they returned, the Boy Jesus lingered behind in Jerusalem. And Joseph and His mother did not know it.*

The word *boy* in the Greek is *pais* and it means a boy often beaten. This doesn't speak of abuse but is describing the ongoing discipline of God into Jesus' life. The Bible says in Hebrews 5:8 that Jesus through suffering and discipline learned how to obey.

> *Though He was a Son, yet He learned obedience by the things which He suffered.*

When we walk with the Father, He is persistently disciplining us so we can come into the maturity that is necessary for His purposes to be fulfilled in us. Just like Jesus, we are often corrected and chastened by the loving hand of God. We must learn to embrace and respond to this as God whispers to us and corrects us to be like Him.

I understand at least somewhat what it is to be disciplined by the Father. As I have walked with the Lord for these decades now, I have come under not only His loving kindness but also the chastening of His hand. When I have paid attention and responded out of the fear of the Lord, it has secured for me a good future. However, if I missed His correction or even disregarded and resisted it, I lived to regret it. This has worked into me a fear of the Lord that I do not want to lose.

One such time was many years ago when Jesus Himself came to me in a dream. Jesus came and stood by me and said these words, "You have grieved the Father." As He spoke these words to me, I knew what I had done, what had allowed me to do it, and what I needed to do to correct it. I look back on this decades later and realize the Lord was correcting in the moment so I wouldn't sabotage the future He had for me. In other words, if I didn't correct this now, it would lead me into a path I didn't want to go. I'm told by airplane pilots that if their settings get off just a little as they fly, the farther they fly the more they get off course. I believe now it was the Lord graciously correcting me to bring me back on course and to let me know that what I thought wasn't a big deal with the Lord actually was.

So often this is what the correcting of the Lord is about. It is letting us know that something really displeases the Lord and is detrimental to His future for us. Otherwise, we tend to dismiss these things and let our own carnality rule and the lust of our flesh. I didn't think of all this then; I only knew I was *in trouble*. What I mean by this is it deeply concerned me that I had grieved the Father. In my dream as Jesus told this to me, I began to weep. I remember being really concerned that I was going to lose the destiny God had for me. As Jesus turned to go back to the Father in my dream—I intuitively knew this was where He was going—I said to Him, "Lord, is this going to cause me to lose my destiny?"

Jesus stopped, turned, and looked at me and said, "I did not come to tell you this so you would be overcome. I came to tell you this so you would overcome." The purpose of the chastening was not to destroy me but empower me to overcome. Wow! If we can understand this, it changes everything. It doesn't make the chastening any more pleasant. In fact, the writer of Hebrews says it's never pleasant in Hebrews 12:11.

> *Now no chastening seems to be joyful for the present, but painful; nevertheless, afterward it yields the peaceable*

fruit of righteousness to those who have been trained by it.

For the moment the chastening we are enduring is not pleasant and even painful. However, when we allow it to work in us, it produces all that God is after. This is the purpose of His correction. This is what I have described God did in me. It caused me to fear the Lord and recognize the way He viewed things I was justifying. It has produced in me hopefully a more yielded heart to the Lord and a walking in the fear of the Lord even as my Father.

There is one more issue we should recognize about the Spirit of adoption. When the Bible speaks of adoption, it is not the same as in our western culture. In Jewish culture when a father adopted a son it wasn't someone from outside the family. The father would literally *adopt* his own son. This was a time in the maturity process of the son when he was now esteemed to be ready to steward the family business, inheritance, and assets. This usually happened at 30 years of age. This is what happened to Jesus at the River Jordan when Jesus was baptized. God officially adopted Jesus and publicly declared Him to be His Son. Mark 1:10-11 is one of the places where this is recorded.

> *And immediately, coming up from the water, He saw the heavens parting and the Spirit descending upon Him like a dove. Then a voice came from heaven, "You are My beloved Son, in whom I am well pleased."*

When the Father's voice from heaven spoke these words, this was the adoption of Jesus taking place. So the Spirit of adoption is not just being accepted into the family. The Spirit of adoption is working in us to prepare us to steward the resources of the Father and His house. We are brought to the place of carrying the responsibility of being a son of our heavenly Father. We are always loved, but once we are adopted we are now commissioned to function on behalf of the Father and the family.

The word *adoption* in the Greek is *huiothesia,* and it means the placing of a son. As the revelation of God as Abba Father comes to us, we are not just settled and secured in His love; we are disciplined then given a place by the Father of function in His kingdom. Paul spoke of this adoption in several places. Romans 9:3-4 shows Paul's passion for the Jewish nation. He even speaks of being lost himself if it would mean Israel being saved.

> *For I could wish that I myself were accursed from Christ for my brethren, my countrymen according to the flesh, who are Israelites, to whom pertain the adoption, the glory, the covenants, the giving of the law, the service of God, and the promises.*

Notice all the things God invested in Israel. One of them was the adoption. I take this to mean that God adopted Israel as His son. Exodus 4:22-23 shows God saying to Pharaoh through Moses that he must let Israel go because he was God's son.

> *Then you shall say to Pharaoh, "Thus says the Lord: 'Israel is My son, My firstborn. So I say to you, let My son go that he may serve Me. But if you refuse to let him go, indeed I will kill your son, your firstborn.'"*

God declares that He will judge harshly that which holds His son in bondage. When we are adopted by the Lord, He rises to defend us. Galatians 4:4-6 shows us that because we are adopted, God sends the Spirit of His Son into our hearts.

But when the fullness of the time had come, God sent forth His Son, born of a woman, born under the law, to redeem those who were under the law, that we might receive the adoption as sons.

And because you are sons, God has sent forth the Spirit of His Son into your hearts, crying out, "Abba, Father!"

As the adoptive sons of God, God sends the Holy Spirit, which is the Spirit of His Son, which is the Spirit of adoption, into our hearts because God has adopted us. When we receive the Holy Spirit, it is a sure sign that we are now the adoptive sons of God. We are ready to be trained by the Spirit to steward the resources of His kingdom. Another scripture that speaks of this adoption is Ephesians 1:5.

Having predestined us to adoption as sons by Jesus Christ to Himself, according to the good pleasure of His will.

Please don't get crazy concerning the whole issue of predestination. No one is being controlled as a puppet on a string. Everyone has a free will to choose to obey or not obey. No one is sentenced to hell and can do nothing about it. Predestination simply means there is a thought-out plan for your life already arranged before you were born. I cover this in my other book on the Courts of Heaven. I like to put it this way. Not only is there a thought-out plan we are in the earth to fulfill through choosing God's will and not our own, but all of heaven is working on our behalf to accomplish it. Notice that we are predestined to the adoption of sons. In other words, all of heaven is working to see us come into the fullness of being His sons. We can't fail when we set our hearts on the Lord. It is a predestined thing to be accomplished and everything in heaven is working on our behalf to see it occur! Take courage. You are going to make it!

I remember being in a service where the worship leader began to sing out what the Great Cloud of Witnesses was speaking over us (see Heb. 12:1). It was an awesome time. As he sang, they were saying, "You're going to make it, you're going to cross the finish line." I cannot tell you what that moment was like. The Cloud of Witnesses from heaven was speaking with all the voices of heaven that we were going to accomplish our purpose. Wow! We may feel like we are struggling at times, but the forces of heaven are standing with us and for us. We are going to make it! We are going to cross the finish line!

A final scripture to mention about adoption is Romans 8:23. We are told the ultimate adoption will be the resurrection from the dead and the total redemption of our bodies.

> *Not only that, but we also who have the firstfruits of the Spirit, even we ourselves groan within ourselves, eagerly waiting for the adoption, the redemption of our body.*

The Spirit of adoption in us is groaning through us desiring the ultimate adoption, which is the redemption of our bodies at the resurrection of the dead. This means that nothing happens by accident or on its own. The Spirit of adoption groaning in travail in intercession is giving birth to the second coming of Jesus so we can have our new bodies. The groaning of the Spirit of adoption through us gives birth to the ultimate event of history. This is amazing. The Spirit of adoption in us is a part of birthing this climatic event. This is why there are times that our intercession may seem to make no sense. We can just come under a burden and travail and not know why. It could be as big as giving birth to the second coming of Jesus and unlocking the event of all history. We need in these times to give place to this and allow the Spirit of adoption in us to have His way.

All of this is connected to God being our Father. When Jesus said, "When you pray, say, Our Father in heaven," He was speaking of an awareness of who God is as our Father and all that is joined to this. The Lord desires to continue to unveil to us His Fatherhood through the Spirit of adoption sent into our hearts. As we approach God as Father, it opens up the first dimension of the Spirit to us. We will discuss this in the next chapter.

CHAPTER 5

THE SECRET PLACE

Remember that each realm of prayer that Jesus taught opens up a dimension of the spirit that we have access into. When Jesus taught us to approach God as our Father, He was aware that we would be able to step into a realm of heaven where things could shift on the earth. Matthew 6:5-6 shows Jesus giving insight into a realm that approaching God as our Father opens to us.

> *And when you pray, you shall not be like the hypocrites. For they love to pray standing in the synagogues and on the corners of the streets, that they may be seen by men. Assuredly, I say to you, they have their reward. But you, when you pray, go into your room, and when you have shut your door, pray to your Father who is in the secret*

place; and your Father who sees in secret will reward you openly.

Jesus lets the disciples know that they aren't to be like the hypocritical religious leaders, who pray to be seen by men. Jesus instructed the disciples to instead go into a room, shut the door, and pray. Notice that as they would do this, they would enter the *secret place*. Jesus is giving them a mystery to prayer in this passage. The *secret place* wasn't the room they were in but a spiritual dimension they entered in the unseen realm. The psalmist spoke of this place in Scripture. Psalm 91:1-2 gives us some insight into this secret place that Jesus is speaking to them about.

He who dwells in the secret place of the Most High
Shall abide under the shadow of the Almighty.
I will say of the Lord, "He is my refuge and my fortress;
My God, in Him I will trust."

Notice that the secret place is a place of dwelling and not just visitation. We are to make it our habitation or where we habitually operate from. Coming into the secret place becomes a part of our lifestyle and not an event. We learn to live in this place in the Spirit and secure the peace, security, and safety that are there for our family and ourselves. When we do, we come under the divine protection of God. We have such an assurance and confidence from this place in the spirit realm that we can boldly declare, "He is my refuge and my fortress; my God, in Him I will trust." We have a divine sense of invincibility because of who the Lord is and the place we have in Him in the spirit.

When you read through Psalm 91, it is amazing the confidence being expressed. We live in such an age of fear. In America alone it is reported that one in six people take psychiatric drugs such as antidepressants or sedatives. This is because of the fear people are living under. Folks are beset by fear on every side and the torment associated with it. Yet the psalmist declares that he is not afraid because of the secret place he lives in with the Lord. Psalm 91:3-8 gives us more assurance of what occurs when we make the secret place our habitation.

> *Surely He shall deliver you from the snare of the fowler*
>
> *And from the perilous pestilence.*
>
> *He shall cover you with His feathers,*
>
> *And under His wings you shall take refuge;*
>
> *His truth shall be your shield and buckler.*
>
> *You shall not be afraid of the terror by night,*
>
> *Nor of the arrow that flies by day,*
>
> *Nor of the pestilence that walks in darkness,*
>
> *Nor of the destruction that lays waste at noonday.*
>
> *A thousand may fall at your side,*
>
> *And ten thousand at your right hand;*
>
> *But it shall not come near you.*
>
> *Only with your eyes shall you look,*
>
> *And see the reward of the wicked.*

All these promises that are ours as we abide in the secret place of the Most High are powerful. We are assured that nothing shall trap us or come on us unexpectedly. We are told what rushes upon humanity will not touch us. We will dwell under His divine protection and security. We won't be afraid at night. Instruments of war will not hurt us or threaten us. No destructive force will be able to harm us. Even when others are perishing around us, it will not be our portion. We will not be a part of the statistics of those who perished. We may see it with our eyes, but it will not affect us or touch us. What precious promises to those who learn to enter the secret place of the Most High God by approaching Him as Father. When we know how to step into this dimension of the spirit realm, we become protected in the natural from all harm. This is because what and where we are in the spirit determines what can touch us in the natural. When we approach God as Father and move into these dimensions, we break the power of fear and live with a confidence in God. Psalm 91:9-13 gives us further insight into the incredible security of living and functioning from the secret place of the Most High God.

> *Because you have made the Lord, who is my refuge,*
>
> *Even the Most High, your dwelling place,*
>
> *No evil shall befall you,*
>
> *Nor shall any plague come near your dwelling;*
>
> *For He shall give His angels charge over you,*
>
> *To keep you in all your ways.*
>
> *In their hands they shall bear you up,*
>
> *Lest you dash your foot against a stone.*
>
> *You shall tread upon the lion and the cobra,*
>
> *The young lion and the serpent you shall trample underfoot.*

As a result of us living from the secret place, we are promised that plagues and evil will not even come close to us. In this secret place, there are angels charged with preserving us from harm and even the slightest injury. We will exercise authority over the powers of the devil from the secret place. When we are making the secret place our habitation, there is a functional authority we will walk in that the devil cannot resist. Lions, cobras, and serpents that represent demonic forces—we will subdue from this place in the spirit realm. Psalm 91:14-16 concludes the psalmist's declaration of what we glean as a result of living in this place in the Spirit.

> *Because he has set his love upon Me, therefore I will deliver him;*
>
> *I will set him on high, because he has known My name.*
>
> *He shall call upon Me, and I will answer him;*
>
> *I will be with him in trouble;*
>
> *I will deliver him and honor him.*
>
> *With long life I will satisfy him,*
>
> *And show him My salvation.*

Notice that living in the secret place is a result of setting our love upon the Lord. We will find that one of the main attributes of this place in the Spirit is intimacy with the Lord. When we love the Lord with our heart, soul, mind, and strength, it allows us entrance into this place. God says that He will deliver us because we are living from this place. He also says He will set us on high or give us places of influence and favor because we have known His name. This means that the secret place is a place where revelation comes to us. The Father begins to show us His secrets when we spend time in the secret place. We gain new revelation that births new dimensions of authority for us to function from.

In this place, we utter a cry to the Lord and we are heard. When we call from this place, God answers. If we should find ourselves in any trouble, the Lord stands with us. He also delivers us from any trouble we might find ourselves subjected to. God will honor us and deliver us because He delights in us. As a result of us living in the secret place of the Most High, God strengthens us to live long-lasting and satisfying lives. His strength is in us and His glory sustains us. During our lifetime, God will over and over show us His saving power and demonstrate His kindness to us for all to see. All of this and more happens because we learn to approach God as Father and live in and function from the secret place.

THE LEADING OF THE HOLY SPIRIT

When Jesus taught us to enter the secret place through approaching God as Father, there are at least three distinct things associated with this. In other words, there are secrets to getting into the secret place. The first thing is we need the leading of the Holy Spirit to help us step into this dimension. Song of Solomon 3:1-5 gives us some insight into entering the secret place.

> *By night on my bed I sought the one I love;*
> *I sought him, but I did not find him.*
> *"I will rise now," I said,*
> *"And go about the city;*
> *In the streets and in the squares*
> *I will seek the one I love."*
> *I sought him, but I did not find him.*
> *The watchmen who go about the city found me; I said,*
> *"Have you seen the one I love?"*
> *Scarcely had I passed by them,*
> *When I found the one I love.*
> *I held him and would not let him go,*
> *Until I had brought him to the house of my mother,*

And into the chamber of her who conceived me.

I charge you, O daughters of Jerusalem,

By the gazelles or by the does of the field,

Do not stir up nor awaken love

Until it pleases.

The bride is searching for her bridegroom and lover. She is wandering the streets trying to find him. She is in a desperate search for the one she loves. This is us seeking to enter the secret place. This is us trying to move into the realm of the spirit where the Lord is. Notice that in her search the watchmen find her. The watchmen are symbolically the prophets or prophetic people. They are the ones who have prophetic insight. Notice that the prophets always find the ones who are seeking the Lord, our Bridegroom. She was not seeking a prophetic word. She was not seeking a prophecy by running to prophetic conference after prophetic conference. She was seeking the One she loved. As a result, the watchmen or prophets *found* her. Her request of the prophets was not for a word. Her request of the prophets was, "Have you seen the One I love?" The prophets always find the one who is seeking the Lover of her soul.

Then an incredible statement is made. It says scarcely or quickly after she left them, she found the One she loved. In other words, the input of the prophetic allowed her to know where to look that she might find the One she loved. Once she found Him, she would not let Him go. This is a picture of our need for prophetic understanding to enter the place where the One we love is. Getting into the secret place and the place of intimacy with Him requires prophetic insight.

I have found this to be true through the years. Every day that I come before the Lord as my Father and seek to enter the secret place, I have to prophetically pay attention to what is happening in the spirit realm. The way I got into the secret place yesterday may not be the way I come into it today. It is imperative that I find my way into it or I will just be doing religious things in prayer. However, if I can come into the secret place, in that place I can present my petitions from intimacy with the Lord and see them answered.

I was ministering for Bishop Joseph Garlington, a wonderful man of God in Pittsburgh, Pennsylvania. I had taught on how to approach God as Father and enter the secret place. As I finished, he came forward and said to his congregation, "Do you know how to enter the secret place?" Knowing Bishop Garlington, they were aware they were about to receive revelation, so they stayed quiet. He then said, "It's a secret!" He proceeded to tell them that we are totally dependent on the Holy Spirit to prophetically lead us into this dimension every day. Just because we got there yesterday in a certain way doesn't mean we will get there today the same way. Just because we sang a certain song in worship that seemed to open that realm in the last service doesn't mean that song will do it in today's service. Every day we must be listening, looking, and sensing our way into the secret place. This makes us completely dependent on the Lord to get us there.

ISOLATION

Having said this, I believe Jesus gave us some secrets in Matthew 6 to approaching God as Father and stepping into the secret place of the Lord. The first thing I see in these verses we previously read is we need to not be afraid of isolation. The corporate gatherings of the church are very important; however, my aloneness with the Lord is essential. Jesus said to go into your room and shut the door. This means the corporate gathering of the church cannot be a substitute for my personal time in His presence.

Many people struggle with this. They like the busyness associated with gatherings and events. Times of being *alone* intimidate them. They might even feel comfortable in corporate prayer times. I know many who claim to be intercessors but it seems never spend time by themselves with the Lord. They are only in gatherings with numbers of people. However, there is a place with God that you can only obtain by yourself. The place of isolation is essential to stepping into the intimate secret place. It is necessary to allow the Lord to rewire you so being *alone* with Him is not a threat but a joy. Many who had radical impacts in the world were fashioned by being alone with God. Moses was on the backside of the desert when God appeared to him from the burning bush. We see this in Exodus 3:1-5.

> *Now Moses was tending the flock of Jethro his father-in-law, the priest of Midian. And he led the flock to the back of the desert, and came to Horeb, the mountain of God. And the Angel of the Lord appeared to him in a flame of fire from the midst of a bush. So he looked, and behold, the bush was burning with fire, but the bush was not consumed. Then Moses said, "I will now turn aside and see this great sight, why the bush does not burn."*
>
> *So when the Lord saw that he turned aside to look, God called to him from the midst of the bush and said, "Moses, Moses!"*
>
> *And he said, "Here I am."*
>
> *Then He said, "Do not draw near this place. Take your sandals off your feet, for the place where you stand is holy ground."*

This encounter with God happens when Moses is alone with a bunch of sheep. He ends up having a dramatic time with God because he is alone. Moses sees a bush burning. This isn't the amazing part. A bush could be on fire because of lightning strikes or other explainable reasons. The amazing part was it wasn't consumed. Of course, what Moses was seeing was the glory of God in this bush. The word *bush* in the Hebrew is *cnah* and it means to prick, a bramble. When you look up the definition of *bramble* it means a prickly scrambling vine or shrub, especially a blackberry or other wild shrub of the rose family. I think this is significant that God chose to reveal Himself to Moses in this *bush*.

The glory of God was in the bush. What was it about this bush that caused God to choose it? First of all, it was available. Moses is on the backside of the desert. There's not a whole lot of anything there but sand, dirt, bushes, and probably snakes and other wild critters. The bush is available. The principle is that God will place His glory upon those who make themselves available. If you want to experience His glory, then come apart and be available. So often it is our busyness that stops us from encountering God and being used by God. If we will separate ourselves unto the Lord and make ourselves available, He will choose us to experience His glory and even be used for His glory. Another thing that stands out to me about this *bush* is it was *scrambling*. This means its nature was to spread out and cover territory. God's glory will come on what has a heart to spread out, influence, and impact. Anything that passionately desires to increase God's rulership and authority will have His glory come on it. Isaiah 9:7 shows us the nature of the kingdom of God.

> *Of the increase of His government and peace*
> *There will be no end,*
> *Upon the throne of David and over His kingdom,*
> *To order it and establish it with judgment and justice*

From that time forward, even forever.

The zeal of the Lord of hosts will perform this.

This is a prophetic declaration over Jesus from the prophet Isaiah. Jesus' kingdom, of which we are a part, will have no end. It will increase until every part of the earth is subdued under its authority. The Lord said He would be zealous to perform and see this done. Anything that has a desire to increase the rule of God will have God's glory come on it. We also see this pattern in Psalm 80:8-11. God likens His people and their influence to a spreading vine.

You have brought a vine out of Egypt;

You have cast out the nations, and planted it.

You prepared room for it,

And caused it to take deep root,

And it filled the land.

The hills were covered with its shadow,

And the mighty cedars with its boughs.

She sent out her boughs to the Sea,

And her branches to the River.

The nature of the people of God is that we are spreading out and taking territory with His influence on our lives. We are to take deep root. So many people never get rooted and placed. If our lives are to have an impact, we must be rooted and placed. John 15:16 tells us that we are to bear remaining fruit.

You did not choose Me, but I chose you and appointed you that you should go and bear fruit, and that your fruit should remain, that whatever you ask the Father in My name He may give you.

111

The word *remain* is the Greek word *meno* and it means to stay in a given place. If we aren't careful, we can get bored, offended, disinterested, and distracted and allow this to cause us to become not rooted. However, to have impact and influence we must be deeply rooted that we might spread out. Not only are we to be rooted in the Lord (see Col. 2:7), but we are to be rightly planted and rooted in our location of assignment. This can mean the city we live in, church we are connected with, apostolic ministry we align to, and other realms of placement. We are to bear fruit in the place we are rooted in and spread out from. In other words, a realm in the earth is changed to look more like heaven because we are there.

Notice also that from this deeply rooted place this vine covers cedars and hills and sends out boughs and branches to the rivers and seas. This is communicating the supernatural element of this vine that is spreading. Cedars speak of people of great influence and authority while hills speak of the positions they occupy. As the spreading bush of God, we are to impact, empower, and influence positions and people of authority. We are to allow them to operate under the shade of our spiritual place. As a result, they can rule righteously and affect powerfully the culture they operate in. We also are to spread out to touch that which is domestic and international. The rivers speak of domestic realms while seas speak of what is international. God is in the process of planting vines that can take deep root so that in the process of generations its influence is felt and released. This all happens because the glory of God comes on what has a heart by nature to spread out.

Another interesting fact about the bramble—it is reported to be wild by nature. I'm constantly amazed that God is not afraid of our wild nature. In fact, He seems to love it. Through society, religion, and other influences there is an attempt to domesticate us. They are threatened by anything that has a wild aspect they cannot control.

Yet God invites that which is wild into His sphere. Romans 11:17 says that we Gentiles, who were wild by nature, were grafted into the vine of God.

> *And if some of the branches were broken off, and you, being a wild olive tree, were grafted in among them, and with them became a partaker of the root and fatness of the olive tree.*

God is not offended by our wild nature. In fact, He desires it. The Jews were very religious and domesticated. They had lost the radical effect it takes to believe God and impact the world. Therefore, they rejected Jesus. On the other hand, the Gentiles were not dominated by religion but were wild. Religion had not controlled them. It had not sucked the wild side from them.

Being wild is not speaking of being unredeemed or of being rebellious. God grafted into the vine that had become domesticated through religion a wild vine. This was so the life that was in the vine could empower that which was still wild and allow it to have an impact. The bottom line is God loves those who are wild in their heart. He loves those who will believe Him with a radical and limitless spirit of faith. They will experience the glory of God because God loves to empower this. If we will believe with radical faith, we will see the glory of God (see John 11:40).

Another thing interesting to me about the bramble that God chose to put His glory in is that it produces blackberries, roses, and other fruitful and beautiful things from what flows through it. God empowers that which is fruitful and makes it even more fruitful. Jesus declared in John 15:8 that God is glorified through much fruit being produced.

By this My Father is glorified, that you bear much fruit;
so you will be My disciples.

The Lord is not looking for just a little fruit, but much fruit. Notice that this declares us to be His disciples. Our lives are to be a demonstration of the nature and glory of the Father through us. As we bear fruit and produce His beauty and fragrance to affect the world, He places His glory in us and on us. The Lord is looking for that which can carry His glory.

This bramble bush also could prick you. This speaks of our humanity, faults, and even failures. This says these things do not disqualify us from carrying the glory of God. Sometimes people are so aware of their weaknesses and frailties they disqualify themselves from the glory of God being on them. However, God is not doing this. We all have that which will stick others at times. They are our imperfections and struggles. Yet God does not allow this to eliminate us. He actually takes our weakness and works brokenness into us from it. The result is the qualification to carry the glory of God. This is what Paul said in Second Corinthians 12:9.

And He said to me, "My grace is sufficient for you, for
My strength is made perfect in weakness." Therefore
most gladly I will rather boast in my infirmities, that the
power of Christ may rest upon me.

The Lord's strength and power are made perfect in our weakness. So God is not looking for our strength but rather for our weakness. Literally our humanity, imperfections, and weaknesses can be used by God to display His glory and honor. This is why God chose the bush to reveal His glory. Another important thing about this bush that God revealed Himself in to Moses was that even though it burned, it was not consumed! The glory of God can be very intense, but it will not consume us; in fact, it will bring life to us. Anytime we are being consumed it is because we are seeking to shine without the glory of God. When we shine and burn because of the glory upon us, we will have impact without burning out. Isaiah 60:1 pronounces we are to arise and shine because God's glory is on us.

> *Arise, shine;*
>
> *For your light has come!*
>
> *And the glory of the Lord is risen upon you.*

When the glory of God is on us, we will burn without being consumed. If we are struggling with burnout, anxiety, and hopelessness, we should ask for the glory of God to come and burn in us. We must repent for attempting to fulfill God's assignment without His empowerment and ask and receive the glory of God into our lives. If God can speak through a burning bush to His chosen vessel, then He can speak through us as well.

This is the last thing I will mention about this bush—God's voice came from it. As Moses approached this bush because it burned and was not consumed, he heard God's voice. If we are to be like this bush and carry God's glory, then His voice must come from us. The world is longing for the prophetic voice of God and doesn't know what they are looking for. We are to be the place where that voice can be encountered. This was spoken prophetically of Jesus in Isaiah 50:4.

> *The Lord God has given Me*
>
> *The tongue of the learned,*
>
> *That I should know how to speak*
>
> *A word in season to him who is weary.*
>
> *He awakens Me morning by morning,*
>
> *He awakens My ear*

To hear as the learned.

Speaking a word in season is a clear depiction of the prophetic. In other words, we know by the Holy Spirit what is happening in the unseen realm and are able to declare it. Notice that the ability to speak a word in season to the weary is a result of hearing correctly. We have the tongue of the learned, or skilled prophetic ministry, because we have the ear of the learned. This is what Jesus said in Matthew 10:27.

> *Whatever I tell you in the dark, speak in the light; and what you hear in the ear, preach on the housetops.*

Jesus said He would tell us things in the dark and we were to speak them in the light. This could be speaking of *dark sayings*. Psalm 78:2 shows the prophet of God declaring he will utter dark sayings.

> *I will open my mouth in a parable;*
>
> *I will utter dark sayings of old,*

Of course, Jesus taught and spoke in parables to the people. These were dark sayings that only the initiated ones who were hungry for God could come to understand. Many times, the prophetic comes in these dark sayings. We hear the words or see the vision yet do not understand the message of them. It takes the revelation of the Spirit to recognize what God is saying. This happened in Scripture in several places. Zechariah as a prophet of God had this occur. Zechariah 4:4-5 shows the prophet seeing olive trees, lampstands, pipes, and oil. The prophet doesn't understand what he is seeing. He asks the angel that is also a part of this encounter.

> *So I answered and spoke to the angel who talked with me, saying, "What are these, my lord?"*
>
> *Then the angel who talked with me answered and said to me, "Do you not know what these are?"*

And I said, "No, my lord."

The angel then begins to explain the significance of what he is seeing. He needed supernatural help to discern the dark saying. *Dark saying* is the Hebrew word *chiydah*. It means a puzzle. It comes from the Hebrew word *chuwd,* which means to tie a knot. A dark saying is a knot we have to untie to understand. This can be the very nature of the prophetic. Jesus says what we hear in the dark, which by the way means in obscurity, we are to proclaim in the light. The dark saying we untie and began to understand in obscurity we then declare into the light for all to hear. This is the prophetic at work.

The word *light* means to shine with rays and to make manifest. As *a bush* used by God, we are to discern the dark sayings of the Lord and be able to declare His mysteries into the earth. This becomes light for others to walk in. Jesus also said what we hear in the ear we should preach from the rooftops. This means the word we hear in the secret place of the Lord we are to preach with authority and influence into culture. Those slight whispers of revelation we receive while with Him have great impact when released publicly. The problem is there are few who will spend time in His presence *alone* to hear in the ear the secrets of the Lord to then declare. Those who do will change the world with His prophetic word. Moses delivered a nation from bondage because in his isolation he had an encounter with God.

Jacob is another who was alone with God and was radically changed. Genesis 32:24-32 records Jacob being by himself and encountering an angel representing God.

> *Then Jacob was left alone; and a Man wrestled with him until the breaking of day. Now when He saw that He did not prevail against him, He touched the socket of his hip; and the socket of Jacob's hip was out of joint as He*

wrestled with him. And He said, "Let Me go, for the day breaks."

But he said, "I will not let You go unless You bless me!" So He said to him, "What is your name?"

He said, "Jacob."

And He said, "Your name shall no longer be called Jacob, but Israel; for you have struggled with God and with men, and have prevailed."

Then Jacob asked, saying, "Tell me Your name, I pray."

And He said, "Why is it that you ask about My name?" And He blessed him there.

So Jacob called the name of the place Peniel: "For I have seen God face to face, and my life is preserved." Just as he crossed over Penuel the sun rose on him, and he limped on his hip. Therefore to this day the children of Israel do not eat the muscle that shrank, which is on the hip socket, because He touched the socket of Jacob's hip in the muscle that shrank.

Jacob encountered God when he was left alone and isolated. In this secret place, several significant things happened to Jacob. Jacob came face to face with God. This implies intimacy. This was up close and personal. Face-to-face encounters with God result in deep changes in us.

I believe this is what happened to Adam after God fashioned and formed him. The Scripture in Genesis 2:7 says God breathed in Adam the breath of life.

*And the Lord God formed man of the dust of the ground,
and breathed into his nostrils the breath of life; and man
became a living being.*

To breathe into someone's nostrils you have to be face to face. God *kissed* Adam to life after He formed him. Intimacy with God was the first thing Adam knew in his life. The word *nostril* is the Hebrew word *aph* and it means nose and face. It also speaks of breathing hard in passion. So when God breathed into Adam life, He put His passion in him. He kissed him with His passion and brought Adam to life. The breath of God in us produces a passion from which we live and function. This was the result of Adam's face-to-face encounter with God. We also see in Second Corinthians 3:18 the effects of having a face-to-face encounter with the Lord.

*But we all, with unveiled face, beholding as in a mirror
the glory of the Lord, are being transformed into the
same image from glory to glory, just as by the Spirit of
the Lord.*

Face-to-face encounters with the Lord in the Spirit change us into His image and likeness. Up until Jacob's face-to-face encounter with the Lord, he was a deceiver, manipulator, and supplanted his way through life. His name actually means a heel grabber or one who would trip another up to get ahead. He lived by his wits and always sought to outfox the next person. He had a great heart to succeed but sought to produce it through whatever means he could. After his encounter with God, his name was changed to Israel, which means he will rule as God. Through the change of his name and therefore character, Jacob, now Israel, was given real authority. Manipulation is always a sign of lack of real authority. This is what people revert to when they want to succeed but don't actually have the authority to produce it.

Notice, however, that the face-to-face encounter that brought the change happened when Jacob was alone in the secret place. Aloneness is absolutely essential to encounters with God that grant new dimensions of authority to rule and succeed from. Another thing that occurred from this encounter while alone was he limped from that day forward. Jacob was so strong, or we might say had such a strong will that had to be broken, that God through the angel had to weaken him. God touched him in his thigh and weakened him so he could be subdued. If we are to be trusted with authority to rule, we must be subdued under the authority of the Lord. Paul understood this principle. He realized that God's strength was made manifest in his weakness. There are times we must be brought to a place of weakness and absolute dependence on the Lord before we can be granted the power to rule. This occurs in the secret place with God when we are alone. Aloneness and isolation are necessary elements of those who will approach God as Father and step into the secret place of the spirit realm.

HE IS YOUR FATHER

Another key to coming into the secret place is to realize He is your Father. He's not just *the* Father, He's *your* Father. Jesus said we should approach and pray to the One who is our personal Father. This means He is concerned about your stuff. He cares about you. First Peter 5:7 tells us we are to cast and throw our cares on Him: *"casting all your care upon Him, for He cares for you."*

The word *care* is the Greek word *merimna*. It means to cause distractions. It comes from the Greek word *merizo* and it means to disunite and divide. If we do not know how to deal with our worries, concerns, anxieties, and troubles, they will serve as distractions to us and cause us to become divided and weakened in our soul and heart. We will feel ourselves pulled in various directions resulting in confusion and discouragement. This is one of the strategies of the devil against us. Very much as it was in the days of Nehemiah when he was rebuilding the walls of Jerusalem, there was much rubbish and confusion. Nehemiah 4:9-10 shows what was happening as a result of much debris.

> *Nevertheless we made our prayer to our God, and because of them we set a watch against them day and night. Then Judah said, "The strength of the laborers is failing, and there is so much rubbish that we are not able to build the wall."*

When there is much *rubbish* to contend with, it can cause a weariness to come on us. We can suffer with lack of motivation and distractions that pulls us away from prayer and the secret places. This is one of the main tools of the devil against the purposes of God. We must become stubborn and set our face as a flint to not be pulled away from the secret place of the Most High God. The devil knows the power we access in these places and wants to keep us out of them at all costs. He will use troubles, pressures, family issues, finances, busyness, and even good things to keep us out of this dimension.

There is a church that I have a great relationship with. This church began to experience a measure of revival. Souls were being saved, healings were manifesting, and people thought unreachable were flocking to this church. There was a great excitement in this community. This church had a good group of intercessors. One by one these intercessors began to be picked off. One got sick. Another had family issues. Still another became upset and left the church. Before it was over, the biggest part of these intercessors were taken out and removed from their position in the spirit world and the secret place. The result was the move of God stalled and church went back to normal. Attendance began to drop. Salvations stopped occurring. The healings and miracles that were drawing the people halted. The pastor became frustrated, confused, and bewildered at it all. The move of God that had been celebrated became a distant memory. This all happened because the devil used the *rubbish* to cause the laborers' strength to fail and intercession to end that which was carrying this budding revival. The bottom line is that intercession from the secret place births revival, sustains revival, and tends revival. The devil knows this and will use the stuff of life to cause distractions to end the prayer lives of the saints. We must be stubborn, resistant, and even violent in our efforts to never let our guard down or stop praying.

Entering the secret place in prayer is absolutely essential to prayers being answered. Prayers that aren't answered outside the secret place will be answered in the secret place. Genesis 1:1-3 gives us some great insight into this principle.

> *In the beginning God created the heavens and the earth. The earth was without form, and void; and darkness was on the face of the deep. And the Spirit of God was hovering over the face of the waters. Then God said, "Let there be light"; and there was light.*

Notice that the earth was void, without form, and in a chaotic state. The Spirit of the Lord began to hover and move over it in this condition. From this hovering presence of God, God spoke and a reordering of creation began to come into place. I heard a very powerful man of God say years ago, "Even God doesn't speak until the Spirit is moving." He then said, "So often we waste our words in prayer before we are in the right place and the Spirit is moving." Words spoken where there is no unction will usually produce nothing. However, if we can step into the secret place of His presence, from that place the same words will bring great results. Smith Wigglesworth, the great healing revivalist said, "I never pray from earth, I always pray from heaven." He was echoing what I am seeking to communicate. We must always pray from the heavenly dimension of the secret place and other spiritual realms to be effective.

One final idea to illustrate this. One morning as I awoke, I became aware that Mary, my wife, was awake and had been awake for quite a while. This is unusual because I am almost always awake and up before her. She then told me she had been up for hours with severe pain in her abdomen. She suspected it was her uterus, ovaries, or other part of the reproductive system. She said the pain and pressure was so bad she had considered getting me up and having me take her to the emergency room. I knew this was serious then, because Mary is not this kind of person who wants to go for medical attention at the drop of a hat. I then said, "Let me pray for you."

She was sitting on the couch and I knelt in front of her and placed my hand on her abdomen and began to pray. I prayed the best prayer I could with faith, boldness, and passion. I was seeking to release the power and anointing of the Lord to heal. When I finished after a few moments I asked if there was any relief. She said, "No."

We talked for a while and then I said, "Let me pray again."

This time I knelt before her, laid my hands on her abdomen, and begin to pray. For whatever reason I was instantly in the spiritual dimension of the secret place. I did nothing different from before. However, this time the presence of God was there. I knew we were before the Lord and in this precious place of His presence and glory. I prayed with an unction that only this dimension allows. I imparted from this dimension the healing life and power of Jesus. When I was through, I asked her what she felt. She instantly said, "The pressure is gone and the pain relieved." She was healed and has had no more recurrences of this condition.

What was the difference from the first prayer to the second one? Very simply, it was where it was offered from. The first one was outside the secret place, while the second one was from the secret place. The result was healing and life flowing into my wife and her condition being healed!

If we are going to be effective in prayer, we must learn to enter these realms of the Holy Spirit. When we do, a lack of results will give way to great results. All because we are learning how to move into the secret place by approaching God as Father. In this place miracles occur and breakthrough comes. In the next chapters we will learn how to step into other realms of the Spirit of God made available to us through the cross of Jesus Christ.

CHAPTER 6

APPROACHING
GOD AS FRIEND

REMEMBER THAT JESUS PLACED PRAYER IN THREE dimensions. We have talked about approaching God as Father and the secret place it opens to us. In this chapter we will look at approaching God as *Friend*. As Jesus taught on prayer in response to the disciples' request to *teach them to pray*, He brought this realm into sight in Luke 11:5-8.

> *And He said to them, "Which of you shall have a friend, and go to him at midnight and say to him, 'Friend, lend me three loaves; for a friend of mine has come to me on his journey, and I have nothing to set before him'; and*

he will answer from within and say, 'Do not trouble me;
the door is now shut, and my children are with me in
bed; I cannot rise and give to you'? I say to you, though
he will not rise and give to him because he is his friend,
yet because of his persistence he will rise and give him as
many as he needs."

This story that Jesus told in response to the disciples' desire to learn to pray is loaded with ideas, concepts, and understanding. First of all, Jesus is revealing that God wants to be our *friend*. What a novel and overwhelming thought. Most of us would be comfortable with the idea that God is our *Father*. However, the familiarity of God being our *friend* would not be a common thought. Yet this clearly is a desire that the Lord has toward us. Jesus would later in John 15:15 actually tell the disciples He considered them His friends.

No longer do I call you servants, for a servant does not
know what his master is doing; but I have called you
friends, for all things that I heard from My Father I have
made known to you.

As a result of their friendship, Jesus promises to tell them secrets from the Father. We will look at this in more detail in a moment. There are others in Scripture who were considered the friends of God. I would say the primary one was Abraham. In three distinct places in Scripture Abraham is called the friend of God. Second Chronicles 20:7 list Abraham as God's friend. It connects Abraham in this capacity causing God to give his descendants a land and an inheritance.

Are You not our God, who drove out the inhabitants
of this land before Your people Israel, and gave it to the
descendants of Abraham Your friend forever?

We see that whoever is considered the friend of God, their descendants are blessed after them. One of the best things we can do for our lineage is to be considered a friend of God. It appears that God rises to protect, defend, and even war on behalf of those and their descendants who are His friends. Isaiah 41:8-10 gives further insight to what it meant for Abraham to be the friend of God.

> *But you, Israel, are My servant,*
>
> *Jacob whom I have chosen,*
>
> *The descendants of Abraham My friend.*
>
> *You whom I have taken from the ends of the earth,*
>
> *And called from its farthest regions,*
>
> *And said to you,*
>
> *"You are My servant,*
>
> *I have chosen you and have not cast you away:*
>
> *Fear not, for I am with you;*
>
> *Be not dismayed, for I am your God.*
>
> *I will strengthen you,*
>
> *Yes, I will help you,*
>
> *I will uphold you with My righteous right hand."*

Notice that Israel was called the servant of God and Jacob considered the chosen of the Lord because Abraham was the friend of God. In other words, being the friend of God caused God to enter into a covenant with Israel. The Lord declared that God would gather them from the farthest regions where they might have been scattered. God's friendship with Abraham stirred His passion toward Israel. Notice they were chosen and not cast away. The Lord promised to strengthen and help them as His people because of Abraham's friendship with Him. When we are the friends of God it promises God will operate in a covenant posture toward us and our lineage after us. One other scripture where the Bible refers to Abraham as God's friend is James 2:23.

> *And the Scripture was fulfilled which says, "Abraham believed God, and it was accounted to him for righteousness." And he was called the friend of God.*

This gives us insight into faith and believing God that brings justification and righteousness. It wasn't Abraham's works that caused God to befriend him; it was his faith in God that stirred the Lord to be his friend. Faith has a very powerful effect upon God. Whoever will exercise real biblical faith sees God's passion toward them invoked. God wants to be this person's friend. This gives us some clear ideas of what God is really looking for. Whoever will choose to operate in faith and believing God is posturing themselves to be God's friend. Whoever believes God, brings pleasure to His heart. Whoever doubts God, causes Him pain. I desire to be one who believes God and brings pleasure to His heart as His friend.

Moses was another one called and considered the friend of God. Exodus 33:9-11 shows Moses being a man who was the friend of God.

> *And it came to pass, when Moses entered the tabernacle, that the pillar of cloud descended and stood at the door of the tabernacle, and the Lord talked with Moses. All the people saw the pillar of cloud standing at the tabernacle door, and all the people rose and worshiped, each man in his tent door. So the Lord spoke to Moses face to face, as a man speaks to his friend. And he would return to the camp, but his servant Joshua the son of Nun, a young man, did not depart from the tabernacle.*

Moses as the friend of God caused the presence and glory of God to descend on the tabernacle. When Moses entered the tabernacle, God came down to commune with His friend. Whoever is a friend of God will attract God's presence. I'm afraid today we have had more value on gifting in the Body of Christ than those who are the friends of God. As one who has traveled extensively, I have seen many highly gifted ministries and people. I have seen few who when they pray, the glory of God comes. I'm afraid there are few who have paid the price to walk as God's friend, where God would come to fellowship with the ones who are really His friends. Notice what the friend of God was able to produce others partook of. The people rose and worshiped in the presence drawn by God's friend. Joshua stayed in the presence of the glory of God after Moses had left. In this glory Joshua was receiving the impartation he would later need to lead Israel into the promised land. All of this was possible because a man who was the friend of God had the ability to see God come as he prayed and worshiped. God spoke to him as a man speaks to his friend. Friends of God have the ability to "create" a presence and glory that others are impacted from.

When someone is a friend of God, we should also know God rises to defend them. When Miriam and Aaron attacked Moses because of him marrying an Ethiopian woman, God rose to protect him. Numbers 12:4-10 shows God's anger being against even Moses' family members that attacked him.

> *Suddenly the Lord said to Moses, Aaron, and Miriam, "Come out, you three, to the tabernacle of meeting!" So the three came out. Then the Lord came down in the pillar of cloud and stood in the door of the tabernacle, and called Aaron and Miriam. And they both went forward. Then He said,*

"Hear now My words:

If there is a prophet among you,

I, the Lord, make Myself known to him in a vision;

I speak to him in a dream.

Not so with My servant Moses;

He is faithful in all My house.

I speak with him face to face,

Even plainly, and not in dark sayings;

And he sees the form of the Lord.

Why then were you not afraid

To speak against My servant Moses?"

So the anger of the Lord was aroused against them, and He departed. And when the cloud departed from above the tabernacle, suddenly Miriam became leprous, as white as snow. Then Aaron turned toward Miriam, and there she was, a leper.

When Aaron and Miriam, the biological brother and sister of Moses, spoke against him, God came down and dealt with it. His question was. "How are you not afraid to speak against one who is My friend and I speak face to face with?" Wow. It is good to be the friend of God because of His protection. We also must be careful not to criticize one who is the friend of God. It is interesting to note that it was not "right" for Moses to marry a woman outside of the Jewish race. Yet God was more upset with those who criticized Moses than Moses marrying an Ethiopian woman. I love what I heard one say years ago: "It wasn't about right or wrong, it was about who was in rulership." God had granted His friend Moses rulership and God came to defend him. When we speak against those in authority and especially those who are the friend of God, we must be very careful. If we touch one who is God's friend, we can suffer the consequences of it. May God help us to walk humbly and surrendered to Him.

When Jesus begins to speak of this realm of prayer of approaching God as Friend, the picture He paints is very important. He speaks of a friend who came on his journey to another friend. Because this friend does not have the means or ability to help him on his journey, he arises at midnight and goes to one of his friends who is wealthy and beseeches him for help. The Scripture says even though this wealthy friend wouldn't rise and help him because he was his friend, he would do it because of his persistence at the midnight hour. In other words, he would get up and give him what he wanted and needed for his other friend so he would go away and let him go back to bed!

In this story we see several key factors. The first thing that stands out to me is the friend who is seeking to get help for the needy friend is *standing between two friends*. He is in the middle between the friend who needs help and the friend who has sufficiency. This is significant. When we approach God as Friend, it is a place of intercession on behalf of others. Anytime we are standing in *the middle* or *in between*, it speaks of a place of intercession. The second thing is the needy friend is on a journey. He is seeking to get to his destination or destiny. When we as friends of God stand in intercession it quite often is seeking to *help* people in the spirit realm to get into the destiny they were made for.

I have a very personal experience in this myself. Years ago when I was 20 or 21 years old, I knew I was called to ministry, but had lost all interest in it. Mary and I were married and had our first child, Ryan. We were just a young married couple doing life. I had no desire to be in ministry and pursue this as a career, occupation, or life for us. I was very much just interested in pursuing my own agenda and desires. Actually, I loved sports. I played basketball, baseball, tennis, and even some golf. I worked a job but played sports in all my time off. It was my passion. This was my first love. I had pretty well set aside any intent to be in ministry or anything like it. I had no longing for it at all.

The *problem* was a group of ladies who met with the pastor's wife once a week for Bible study. They would have their teaching time then spend time in prayer. I was later told they would begin to pray and this intense intercession and travail would come over the group concerning me and ministry. They said they would cry out to God to deliver me from *sports* and restore me to my first love, Jesus. I did not know any of this was happening. As a result of their constant and intense prayers for me as the friends of God, God came after me. This was when He entered my car without invitation and unannounced and began the process of executing His call and agenda for my life. I am in the ministry today because these friends of God prayed me out of that which held me and into my destiny! Their travail as God's friends secured from heaven my purpose and destiny. I still stand in amazement at this almost forty years later. God is looking for friends who can take up the case of others before Him. People who are to be used by God need the friends of God to stand on their behalf before the Lord.

Abraham did this on behalf of Sodom and Gomorrah. Genesis 18:16-33 shows the interaction of Abraham as the friend of God. Remember that the Scriptures are clear that Abraham was considered the friend of God.

> *Then the men rose from there and looked toward Sodom, and Abraham went with them to send them on the way. And the Lord said, "Shall I hide from Abraham what I am doing, since Abraham shall surely become a great and*

mighty nation, and all the nations of the earth shall be blessed in him? For I have known him, in order that he may command his children and his household after him, that they keep the way of the Lord, to do righteousness and justice, that the Lord may bring to Abraham what He has spoken to him." And the Lord said, "Because the outcry against Sodom and Gomorrah is great, and because their sin is very grave, I will go down now and see whether they have done altogether according to the outcry against it that has come to Me; and if not, I will know."

Then the men turned away from there and went toward Sodom, but Abraham still stood before the Lord. And Abraham came near and said, "Would You also destroy the righteous with the wicked? Suppose there were fifty righteous within the city; would You also destroy the place and not spare it for the fifty righteous that were in it? Far be it from You to do such a thing as this, to slay the righteous with the wicked, so that the righteous should be as the wicked; far be it from You! Shall not the Judge of all the earth do right?"

So the Lord said, "If I find in Sodom fifty righteous within the city, then I will spare all the place for their sakes."

Then Abraham answered and said, "Indeed now, I who am but dust and ashes have taken it upon myself to speak to the Lord: Suppose there were five less than the fifty righteous; would You destroy all of the city for lack of five?"

So He said, "If I find there forty-five, I will not destroy it."

And he spoke to Him yet again and said, "Suppose there should be forty found there?"

So He said, "I will not do it for the sake of forty."

Then he said, "Let not the Lord be angry, and I will speak: Suppose thirty should be found there?"

So He said, "I will not do it if I find thirty there."

And he said, "Indeed now, I have taken it upon myself to speak to the Lord: Suppose twenty should be found there?"

So He said, "I will not destroy it for the sake of twenty."

Then he said, "Let not the Lord be angry, and I will speak but once more: Suppose ten should be found there?"

And He said, "I will not destroy it for the sake of ten." So the Lord went His way as soon as He had finished speaking with Abraham; and Abraham returned to his place.

God seems to be asking Himself a question. Should He tell Abraham what He is about to do to Sodom and Gomorrah? Should He let Abraham, His friend, in on the secret that Sodom and Gomorrah are about to be destroyed because of their wickedness? Clearly the Lord decides it is something Abraham should know. There was a hidden agenda God had in telling His friend Abraham what was about to happen. The Lord knew that Abraham as His friend would know the heart of God was to show mercy. It's interesting that God doesn't *tell* Abraham to ask Him for mercy for Sodom and Gomorrah. God knows that Abraham as His friend will know this is the passion of God. Abraham is able to read between the lines and discern that God's heart was for someone to give Him the right He needed to be merciful to this city's wickedness. We see this is other portions of Scripture. Ezekiel 22:29-31 gives a glaring view of what God desires to do and what God *had* to do.

> *"The people of the land have used oppressions, committed robbery, and mistreated the poor and needy; and they wrongfully oppress the stranger. So I sought for a man among them who would make a wall, and stand in the gap before Me on behalf of the land, that I should not destroy it; but I found no one. Therefore I have poured out My indignation on them; I have consumed them with the fire of My wrath; and I have recompensed their deeds on their own heads," says the Lord God.*

God did not want to destroy and judge, but because no one gave him a reason to be merciful, His indignation was poured out. There must be friends of God who can sense His heart and seek to give Him the reason He is looking for to show mercy and kindness instead of judgment and even destruction. This is what Abraham was doing when He began with fifty and went down to ten righteous. The Lord agreed that if there were ten righteous, for their sakes God will not judge Sodom and Gomorrah. Abraham was doing the very same thing that Jesus said the friends of God would do on behalf of their other friends in Luke 11. Abraham was standing between God and Sodom and Gomorrah and seeking to broker a deal of mercy for this undeserving people. He was able to do it before the Lord his Friend, but what they agreed on could not be found. Yet if there had been ten righteous, history would have been completely different.

Another big issue in this story is that Abraham was praying from *secrets* revealed to him from God. No one else on the planet knew what was about to happen to Sodom and Gomorrah but Abraham. From this encounter with God, Abraham became aware of the impending doom looming over this region. He had a secret from God that he alone on the earth knew. This again is what Jesus said those who were His friends would be privy to. Remember that He said, "Everything the Father is showing me, I am telling you." In other words, you have secrets others don't know. This is one of the chief things that says we are the friends of God. Psalm 25:14 tells us one of the groups that are privy to the *secrets* of God.

> *The secret of the Lord is with those who fear Him,*
> *And He will show them His covenant.*

When we walk in the fear of the Lord and order our lives accordingly, God shares His secrets with us. He is looking for those in the earth to whom He can reveal what is happening so they can partner with Him for His will to be done in the midst of it. Let me explain it this way. God tells His friend Abraham a secret of immense magnitude that no one else knows. Sodom and Gomorrah are going to be destroyed. I tell people sometimes that if God had shared that inside information with me, I would have prophesied it and become famous when it happened. All the TV stations, newspapers, websites, etc. would have wanted me. I would have been known as the one who forecasted one of the most crucial events in history before it happened. I could have parlayed that into wealth, fame, and influence. People would have listened to me from that time on because I was the prophet who spoke what really did happen. There's only one problem. The secret God told Abraham was not so he could prophesy from it, but so he could pray from it.

This is the mistake we make as the friends of God at times. We think because we know secrets, we are to prophesy them in public. Maybe we are being told so we can pray from them in private. I have learned this not only from Scripture but from my own experience. In early 2008 I had a dream where I saw the Dow Jones market in the form of a thermometer. It was very high. I then watched as it dropped in a terrifying fall. There was a line on the gauge. I intuitively knew as I watched this that if it dropped below that line it would be destroyed and would not recover. It came very close to that line in its drop. Even though I couldn't tell with the naked eye if it had gone below this non-recoverable point, I knew it hadn't. It was close but had not declined to this level. I also knew that the market would go back up and whoever was rightly positioned would make a lot of money. I knew all this as I watched it in my dream. I was aware I was being shown an economic crash that would have devastating effects. It was a secret from the Lord about something that was coming.

I had had these kinds of things before with regard to financial matters. I knew what I was seeing could be trusted. I felt I must warn and prophesy what I had seen and let people protect themselves from the consequences that were coming. But I knew I did not have a sufficient enough platform to get this word out. This made me wonder why God had shown it to me in the first place. Why show me something I can do nothing about? This was my question. I soon after was in a meeting with some influential leaders in the Body of Christ. I thought, "These people can get the word out, or maybe grant me a platform to get it out." I told them my dream. To my utter shock and dismay, not only did they not accept and receive it, they laughed at me. I remember one actually mocking and saying, "Robert thinks the stock market is going to crash," then all of them laughing about it. I suddenly felt very small. It wasn't a good experience. I was further confused on why God would show me such a thing with nowhere to take it.

Of course, in hindsight we know that what I saw did in fact happen. In late 2008, the market began to plummet. It fell throughout the rest of the year and into early 2009. In March 2009 after the fall through the last quarter of 2008, its lowest point was 6,443.27. Then just as I had seen over the course of time, it began to go back up. At this writing today, the market is at an historic rise and level. It closed at 25,250.55. *Wow!* The stock market did in fact recover, but not until after great pain and destruction to many, many lives.

Here's the question. Why did God show this to me? I clearly had no way to *prophesy* it with any real effectiveness. Why would God show me a secret with nothing to do about it? I didn't know at that time what I know now. When something was revealed to me then, I always thought it was so I could prophesy it into the public. I now know that just like Abraham, it was so I could pray from it in secret. Abraham took the revelation he had from God and began to interceded as the friend of God on behalf of a doomed people. Through his intercession, he brokered a deal with God to spare this people if ten righteous could be found. If the ten righteous had been found in this city/region, the intercession of Abraham from a secret revealed by God would have changed history.

History can be dictated by the friends of God who know their place before Him. Maybe we could not have stopped the financial fallout from the crash of the market, but I believe we could have altered its effect to some degree. For instance, Jesus in Matthew 24:20 tells His disciples that when tribulation and destruction comes, they should pray and alter the way it touches them.

And pray that your flight may not be in winter or on the Sabbath.

Jesus didn't tell them to pray and stop what was coming in A.D. 70. However, He did advise them to pray so that the time might be adjusted. As a result, the effect against them could be altered and changed. I believe in the case of the 2008 economic crash that if I had understood as the friend of God that I was shown a secret of what was

138

coming, I could have stood before the Lord and adjusted its effect on perhaps the Body of Christ or even beyond. We might not have been able to prevent it, but we could have rearranged it enough in the spirit world that its effect could have been lessened.

There are many secrets that God would want to reveal to those who are His friends. From these secrets we are not necessarily called to prophesy. Most of us will not have a platform to do that from that would have any real effect. But we can take the secret and pray from it to alter and even prevent some things from happening. We can change the course of events that will adjust things that will give us a different future. What a tremendous opportunity God has given to us as His friends. In the next chapter we will look into the realm of the Spirit that approaching God as Friend opens up. It's quite amazing. I'm excited just thinking about it.

CHAPTER 7

THE COUNCIL
OF THE LORD

JUST LIKE APPROACHING GOD AS FATHER OPENS THE SECRET place, approaching God as His friend also opens up a spiritual place we can stand in. It is called the *Council of the Lord*. Jeremiah referred to this realm in Jeremiah 23:18.

> *For who has stood in the counsel of the Lord,*
>
> *And has perceived and heard His word?*
>
> *Who has marked His word and heard it?*

The Council of the Lord is a place in the spirit world. The friends of God are those who have access into this realm. In the Old

Testament, primarily the prophets could access this place. It was in this place that they heard the word of the Lord. This is what Jeremiah is referring to.

He is combatting the false prophets of his day. The point he is making is if you are a real prophet you will have stood in the Council of the Lord. In the Old Testament only prophets had access there. Prophets were the friends of God who were invited into this place of this spirit dimension. Jeremiah is challenging the supposed "prophets" of his day with the fact that they know nothing of the Council of the Lord. The verses leading up to Jeremiah 23:18 declare this. Jeremiah 23:16-17 outright challenges the validity of the words of these prophets.

> *Thus says the Lord of hosts:*
>
> *"Do not listen to the words of the prophets who prophesy to you.*
>
> *They make you worthless;*
>
> *They speak a vision of their own heart,*
>
> *Not from the mouth of the Lord.*
>
> *They continually say to those who despise Me,*
>
> *'The Lord has said, "You shall have peace";*
>
> *And to everyone who walks according to the dictates of his own heart, they say,*
>
> *'No evil shall come upon you.'"*

Wow! Jeremiah is saying because these supposed prophets have not been in the Council of the Lord, they are speaking from their own hearts. They are speaking worthless words. Their words are not coming from the mouth of the Lord. They have not been in the Council of the Lord where the real word of the Lord is heard and the real word of the Lord is marked. As a result of this, they are giving the people false hope and promises. We must have people who are the friends of God who can stand in the Council of the Lord. Some amazing things occur as God's friends stand in this place. Our activity in this dimension as God's friends can shift things in the natural realm into divine order. Breakthroughs will be the result of God's friends standing in His Council. Before we go into what can happen in this Council, let me show you the rights we have as a New Testament people.

It is true that only the prophets were allowed as the friends of God to stand in the Council of the Lord. We see Abraham as God's friend and prophet standing there. Genesis 18:22 shows Abraham standing before the Lord. This means that as he interceded for Sodom and Gomorrah, he did it from the Council of the Lord.

> *Then the men turned away from there and went toward Sodom, but Abraham still stood before the Lord.*

Anytime we see the word *stood* we should consider that it is speaking of someone standing in the Council of the Lord. As we will see later, Elijah stood there, Isaiah stood there, Moses stood there, and Micaiah stood there. All these are Old Testament prophets who were allowed by God to stand in His Council. However, the good news for us is that as New Testament believers we have been granted access into this dimension that only a handful could access in the Old Testament. This is actually why Peter spoke of the prophecy of Joel in Acts 2:14-18.

> *But Peter, standing up with the eleven, raised his voice and said to them, "Men of Judea and all who dwell in Jerusalem, let this be known to you, and heed my words. For these are not drunk, as you suppose, since it is only*

the third hour of the day. But this is what was spoken by the prophet Joel:

'And it shall come to pass in the last days, says God,

That I will pour out of My Spirit on all flesh;

Your sons and your daughters shall prophesy,

Your young men shall see visions,

Your old men shall dream dreams.

And on My menservants and on My maidservants

I will pour out My Spirit in those days;

And they shall prophesy.'"

Peter was declaring that something magnificent had just occurred. A transition from the Old Testament had happened. As of the moment the Holy Spirit came into the upper room, God's desire for all His people to be prophetic was enacted. The Holy Spirit, who produces the prophetic, was now coming on all the people of God. The realm of the Spirit, which only the prophets were able to enter in the Old Testament, was now accessible to all who were the Lord's. To dream dreams, see visions, and prophesy requires standing in the Council of the Lord. Remember, Jeremiah said only those who stand in the Council of the Lord hear His word and mark His word. By the way, the word *mark* means to prick up the ears. It's the idea of listening intently even with the fear of the Lord on us. In the Council of the Lord, it is a place of listening intently. As New Testament believers filled with the Holy Spirit, we have a prophetic nature and abilities that allow us as the friends of God to stand in the Council of the Lord. From this dimension of the Council of the Lord as His, friend things move on the earth.

There are several things that can occur from the Council of the Lord as we stand in this holy place of the heavens. Remember that we all have varying prophetic abilities in the Spirit realm. These prophetic abilities will determine how we function in the Council of the Lord. For instance, I have great friends who are terrific seers. Their primary means of prophetic activity is by seeing into the spirit world. Others are great hearers. Some are feelers in the spirit dimensions.

For me personally, if I was to categorize the way I receive spiritual information, it would be first as a feeler, second as a hearer, and third as a seer. I can operate in all of them but feeling is the strongest. I have learned by faith as I pray to sense where I am in the spirit world. As I sense/feel I can determine where I am and what I should be doing at this time. I do all this through faith. Because I have a revelation from the Word of God concerning the Council, I can by faith set my heart and begin to function there prophetically as the friend of God. I have seen good things happen from the Council as I by faith take my place there as the friend of God.

I have discovered that I can pray about a lot of things, but when I approach the Lord based on divine assignments given me, it ushers me into this dimension of the spirit. In other words, it is possible to have divine assignments that require us to stand in the Council of the Lord. As I seek to obey the mandate connected to an assignment, I will immediately be standing in the Council of the Lord.

For instance, at the time of this writing I have a divine assignment to stand in the Council on behalf of the United States President, Donald J. Trump. In March 2016 when the U.S. was in the heat of the primaries for President, I had a dream. At the time of this dream there were still ten or more candidates on the Republican side running for the office of President. In my dream Donald Trump called me on the phone and wanted me to hold a conference to shift things for him concerning the election. The conference was to be held on July 6th. I looked up July 6th and was shocked to find that the Republican Party was birthed on July 6, 1854. What are the chances? As I discovered this, I felt I heard the Lord say, "I want to reclaim the Republican Party for My purposes."

This is what we have been contending for since that time. However, my first assignment was to get things arranged in the spirit world so Donald Trump could take his God-appointed place as President of the United States. We did in fact schedule and host this conference. In preparation for the conference, I felt the Lord tell me that there would be a point in the conference when I would be invited into the Council of the Lord. At this time, I didn't really know if there was a difference between the Council of the Lord and the Courts of Heaven. I now know they are similar yet a different place in the spirit realm. I will talk about the differences later in this book. At the time of the conference, however, I was just doing what I felt, heard, and saw in the spirit world. On Friday night of the conference I was aware that I was being invited to stand in the Council on behalf of Donald Trump and his candidacy for President. The Lord had said to me that when I stood in the Council I must decree James 1:11.

For no sooner has the sun risen with a burning heat than it withers the grass; its flower falls, and its beautiful appearance perishes. So the rich man also will fade away in his pursuits.

In obedience to this word I stood by faith on that stage in the natural, but standing in the Council of the Lord in heaven. I began to declare, "Hillary Clinton's campaign is as grass and she is as the flower of the grass and I say that the burning, searing, exposing heat of God will cause her and her campaign to wither away. I also decree from this place in the spirit world that Donald J. Trump will be seated as the President of the United States."

Of course, we all know what happened. Clinton's campaign did in fact wither away. There was an FBI investigation only two weeks before the election that still boggles the mind to this day as to why it was done by an agency whose leadership clearly wanted her to win. The only explanation is that from the Council of the Lord a judgment was rendered against her and her campaign. The result is Donald Trump became the President of the United States.

However, my time in the Council of the Lord on behalf of now-President Donald J. Trump did not end there. I had a second dream after his election. In this dream, now-President Donald J. Trump came and asked me to be a part of his cabinet and administration. I knew I was being invited into the Council of the Lord on behalf of his presidency and administration. My assignment was to stand in the spirit world and from the Council of the Lord set things in order for him to accomplish in the natural what he is to do. Every time I would begin to pray in agreement with this assignment, I would suddenly be standing in the Council of the Lord. My assignment granted me audience there on behalf of President Donald J. Trump.

I then had a third dream. In this dream President Trump came and asked me to be his *running mate* for a second term. This was right after the inauguration for his first term. At this writing I am *running* with him in the spirit realm to set and keep things in order for him to finish his first term and be re-elected to the second. When I asked why I would be having such a dream when he was just starting his first term, the Lord said to me, "What I intend to do through him will require two terms as the United States President." Again at this writing we continue to contend from the Council of the Lord for God's will to be done in these matters.

I cite these examples of functioning in the Council of the Lord in its effect upon a nation. God needs friends who will stand before Him and represent leaders and nations before Him. As I have stood in the Council of the Lord in these assignments, the Lord also told me to refer to the President as "Donald J. Trump, my president." As I pondered why this was important, I felt the Lord said, "Because as my friend you have a place before Me that allows Me to bless and move on behalf of that which is yours." I know that can come across as arrogant, but this is exactly what happened to Abraham as God's friend on behalf of Sodom and Gomorrah. God did for Abraham as His friend what He wouldn't do for others. When I refer to the President as *Donald J. Trump my president*, it is giving God the right to move because it's mine. God will do for His friends what He will not do for others.

The other thing I would mention is it was important to call him "Donald J. Trump." In the apostolic prophetic movement at the time there were those who were pushing for the president to be more a "John" than a "Donald." The J stands for "John." They felt President Trump *needed* to be a *John,* which means *beloved.* I've never agreed with this. The religious leaders think we need a "John," the beloved who will reflect this from the Lord. My opinion is we don't need this. "Donald" actually means "world ruler." The assignment on Donald J. Trump's life is *not* to be the "beloved." His assignment is to change the world and set things in order. I believe God had me declaring "my President, Donald J. Trump" because by saying "my," God could do it for me and by declaring him as "Donald," I was releasing this dimension of his character and call. I was told to say "J" because he will be the beloved but it will not override his primary assignment, which is to dismantle the demonic agenda that has been moving for decades now. He will not do it, however, without those who can stand in the Council of the Lord on behalf of him and his administration. I believe if we can stand in this place as the friends of God, we can shift nations into divine order!

There are at least five things we can do when we stand in the Council of the Lord. I'm sure these are not exhaustive but are simply some insights to what the Holy Spirit might lead and empower us to operate in from this place of the Spirit. Before I go into these five things, let me say that we have evidence in the New Testament of these places in the spirit realm where people found themselves. The apostle Paul was probably referring to this dimension when he spoke of himself or another who was caught up into the third heaven. Second Corinthians 12:2-4 speaks of *a man* who had a heavenly experience.

> *I know a man in Christ who fourteen years ago—whether in the body I do not know, or whether out of the body I do not know, God knows—such a one was caught up to the third heaven. And I know such a man—whether in the body or out of the body I do not know, God knows—how he was caught up into Paradise and heard inexpressible words, which it is not lawful for a man to utter.*

Most believe Paul was speaking of himself in this account. Notice that he was uncertain of whether he was in his body or out of his body. He just knew he had a heavenly experience in the third heaven. The third heaven is speaking of the Throne Room of God that we read about in other places of Scripture. It would be what most would be referring to when they speak of *heaven*. Paul said this *place* was so glorious and astounding that he heard inexpressible words and things that it isn't right to speak of in this life. This was probably the Council of the Lord or something closely related to it. We see this place also spoken of in First Kings 22:19-22 when Micaiah, a prophet of the Lord, is summoned to the courts of Ahab. When he is asked what the Lord is saying concerning a battle Ahab is going into, he responds with his account in the Council of the Lord where decisions are made about even the destinies of nations and leaders.

> *Then Micaiah said, "Therefore hear the word of the Lord: I saw the Lord sitting on His throne, and all the host of heaven standing by, on His right hand and on His left. And the Lord said, 'Who will persuade Ahab to go up, that he may fall at Ramoth Gilead?' So one spoke in this manner, and another spoke in that manner. Then a spirit came forward and stood before the Lord, and said, 'I will persuade him.' The Lord said to him, 'In what way?' So he said, 'I will go out and be a lying spirit in the mouth of all his prophets.' And the Lord said, 'You shall persuade him, and also prevail. Go out and do so.'"*

The Lord made His decision about how Ahab would fall and the change of leadership of a nation. This was done in the Council of the Lord. Micaiah as a prophet was given entrance into this place of the spirit realm and allowed perhaps even input. He saw what was going to happen as determined from the Council of God.

We may not have these kinds of awesome experiences in this dimension. However, by faith we can stand in these places in the spirit world. It seems that Hebrews 12:22-24 is also describing these places that we as New Testament people have access into.

> *But you have come to Mount Zion and to the city of the living God, the heavenly Jerusalem, to an innumerable company of angels, to the general assembly and church of the firstborn who are registered in heaven, to God the*

Judge of all, to the spirits of just men made perfect, to
Jesus the Mediator of the new covenant, and to the blood
of sprinkling that speaks better things than that of Abel.

Even though I believe this is also speaking of the Courts of Heaven that we will get to in later chapters, I believe it is also revealing the Council of the Lord. Remember that the Courts of Heaven and the Council of the Lord, though different places in the spirit world, are closely related. My reason for citing this scripture here is to show us that as New Testament believers we have access into what only the prophets did in the Old Testament. We have a right by the blood of Jesus to stand in these places of the Spirit and see things shift in the natural world. The writer is expressing much of the spiritual activity that is happening in the unseen realm in this scripture. We have been granted access into these places and should know how to function there. There are angels, the general assembly of worshipers, the Judge Himself, the Cloud of Witnesses, the Mediator Jesus, and even the blood speaking in these places. This is pretty mystical and spiritual, but it is the place we have been permitted and encouraged to function in and from by faith. We may not wonder are we *in the body or out of the body*, but by faith because of what Scripture teaches we can stand in these places and sense their atmosphere. We can walk by faith and not by sight and engage these dimensions of the heavenly realm.

When we step into the atmosphere of the Council of the Lord, we can receive counsel or wisdom. Many times as believers, we need to have understanding and wisdom from the Lord. James 1:5-8 tells us that we should ask for wisdom from the Lord. He desires to give us insight into situations and answers for them from His Council.

If any of you lacks wisdom, let him ask of God, who gives
to all liberally and without reproach, and it will be given

to him. But let him ask in faith, with no doubting, for he who doubts is like a wave of the sea driven and tossed by the wind. For let not that man suppose that he will receive anything from the Lord; he is a double-minded man, unstable in all his ways.

God clearly loves to grant wisdom to those who ask Him. Proverbs 2:6 declares that wisdom, knowledge, and understanding come from the *mouth* of the Lord.

For the Lord gives wisdom;

From His mouth come knowledge and understanding.

Wisdom is not just learning certain principles and statutes. Wisdom comes from hearing the voice of the Lord. We know because of Jeremiah 23:18 that in the Council of the Lord we *hear His word and mark His word.* So as we enter the Council of the Lord, God can speak His wisdom and secrets to us concerning issues of our lives or others. He gives to us liberally and without any form of reproach or defamation. He doesn't chide us for not knowing something. In fact, He is delighted when we come in our weakness and ask for His wisdom. However, notice that we must come in faith and be single-hearted to receive from Him. If we allow doubt to cause us to waver in our asking, we will not get anything from Him. We must be focused and sincere in our asking. When we approach Him and His Council with this attitude, from this place in the spirit realm God's wisdom and secrets concerning a matter can be revealed. This wisdom will actually solve problems, bring success, and give direction for us to walk in. This comes from the Council of the Lord as we enter it by approaching God as our Friend.

In the Council of the Lord we can also give counsel to God. This may come as a great surprise. In this realm of the Spirit we not only receive from the Council of God, but the Lord actually allows us to counsel Him. This initially may seem very presumptuous until we realize this is what both Abraham and Moses did as the friends of God. When Abraham became aware of the intent of God to destroy Sodom and Gomorrah, he asked God a question. Genesis 18:24-25 shows Abraham through a question reminding God of who He is. In this, he gives God counsel.

> *Suppose there were fifty righteous within the city; would You also destroy the place and not spare it for the fifty righteous that were in it? Far be it from You to do such a thing as this, to slay the righteous with the wicked, so that the righteous should be as the wicked; far be it from You! Shall not the Judge of all the earth do right?*

Abraham counsels the Lord concerning His activities with this wicked place. He reminds God that as the *Judge of all the earth* He couldn't and shouldn't destroy the righteous with the wicked. In fact, Abraham is counseling the Lord through prayer. He did it with great reverence, honor, and fear, but he brought to the attention of God this awareness. When we know how to stand in the Council of the Lord, we can with great humility yet boldness plead for the case of others. We need to know the protocol of these dimensions so we know how to behave ourselves in these holy places. Abraham knew God's heart and petitioned Him on this basis. He persuaded the Lord in this spiritual arena to show mercy based on any righteous who would be there. Abraham was aware that God never wanted the punishment of the wicked to land on the righteous. We see this in Psalm 125:3:

> *For the scepter of wickedness shall not rest*
> *On the land allotted to the righteous,*

Lest the righteous reach out their hands to iniquity.

The word *scepter* is the Hebrew word *shebet*. It means to branch off. It speaks of a stick for punishing, correcting, and other aspects of ruling. God is declaring that He will not allow the righteous to come under the abusive rulership of the wicked but also that the righteous would not suffer the punishment of the wicked. The thought is clear. If they did, the righteous would become discouraged and disillusioned and begin to sin and put their hands to unrighteousness. They would see no reason to live holy if they are going to suffer the same retribution as those who didn't. From this simple concept, Abraham is reminding God and counseling God about His activities in Sodom and Gomorrah. God cannot leave the impression in His dealings with Sodom and Gomorrah that it doesn't pay to be righteous. Abraham is being jealous for the Name and reputation of the Lord. He is showing passion concerning what people will think of the Lord for generations to come. From this place God is willing to receive counsel from Abraham about His intent in Sodom and Gomorrah. He agrees with what Abraham is proposing. We too can stand in this place with God on behalf of issues in the earth. We can learn to operate in the protocol of the Council of heaven and see God's heart moved. What an awesome privilege we have been extended.

Moses also stood in the Council of the Lord in Numbers 14:11-23. In these scriptures we see Moses convincing God to spare the nations of Israel and not wipe them out.

> *Then the Lord said to Moses: "How long will these people reject Me? And how long will they not believe Me, with all the signs which I have performed among them? I will strike them with the pestilence and disinherit them, and I will make of you a nation greater and mightier than they."*

And Moses said to the Lord: "Then the Egyptians will hear it, for by Your might You brought these people up from among them, and they will tell it to the inhabitants of this land. They have heard that You, Lord, are among these people; that You, Lord, are seen face to face and Your cloud stands above them, and You go before them in a pillar of cloud by day and in a pillar of fire by night. Now if You kill these people as one man, then the nations which have heard of Your fame will speak, saying, 'Because the Lord was not able to bring this people to the land which He swore to give them, therefore He killed them in the wilderness.' And now, I pray, let the power of my Lord be great, just as You have spoken, saying, 'The Lord is longsuffering and abundant in mercy, forgiving iniquity and transgression; but He by no means clears the guilty, visiting the iniquity of the fathers on the children to the third and fourth generation.' Pardon the iniquity of this people, I pray, according to the greatness of Your mercy, just as You have forgiven this people, from Egypt even until now."

Then the Lord said: "I have pardoned, according to your word; but truly, as I live, all the earth shall be filled with the glory of the Lord—because all these men who have seen My glory and the signs which I did in Egypt and in the wilderness, and have put Me to the test now these ten times, and have not heeded My voice, they certainly shall not see the land of which I swore to their fathers, nor shall any of those who rejected Me see it."

God is very upset with this people who have perpetually resisted His goodness and desire. When He finally gets them to the border of the promised land and they are ready to cross over, they rebel. This is the final straw for the Lord after He has shown them His faithfulness and power time after time. They have habitually turned back in their hearts and God is done. He tells Moses to get away from them because He is going to destroy the whole lot of them. He will then raise up from Moses another nation. Moses instead comes and stands in the Council of the Lord before Him. He begins to remind God that this isn't a good idea.

He points out to the Lord that should He do this, all will say that God was strong enough to bring them out of Egypt but not strong enough to bring them to the land of Canaan. This will be a blemish on the Name of the Lord for generations to come. On the basis of God's reputation in the earth, Moses appeals to God. God relents in what He has said He will do and instead shows Israel mercy again. How did Moses stand before the Lord and bring advice into His Council? There is one powerful thing that caused God to *hear* Moses in this place. It is that Moses had a jealousy for God and His purposes in the earth. Moses had become so pregnant with a passion to see God glorified and His will fulfilled. Even when God offered to make Moses a great nation that would take the place of this people, Moses declined. He was more interested in God's stuff than anything for himself. This can only occur when we have allowed the heart of God to be worked into our lives. His passion possesses us more than any desire of our own. This equips us to stand in this place called the Council of the Lord.

Moses seeks the Lord on behalf of Israel on the basis of God's reputation and His Name in the earth. God agrees to do what Moses is suggesting. He shows mercy and makes a powerful statement to Moses. He says to Moses, *"I have pardoned them according to your word."* Wow! God shows Israel mercy because of the intercession of Moses on behalf of this nation in the Council of the Lord. This is the power of having a place as the friend of God in the Council of the Lord. God then makes it clear that the *knowledge of the glory of the Lord will cover the earth*. In other words, God will be jealous for His Name and not allow any blemish to be attached to it. The glory of who He is will be seen.

Moses successfully gave counsel to the Lord and saw a nation spared from destruction. We too can stand in the Council of the Lord as His friend and secure blessings and mercies for ourselves, our families, all the way up to nations. God is looking for these who can take their place there and grant Him the right to be merciful in situations in the earth. What an awesome place we have been given before the Lord of glory.

In and from the Council of the Lord we can make decisions with God concerning things in the earth. This is what Abraham did with God concerning Sodom and Gomorrah. Abraham began with asking if 50 righteous could be found, would God spare this wicked place? He ended with God agreeing that ten would be sufficient for this people to be shown mercy. Genesis 18:24-26 shows the beginning of this dialogue that Abraham had with God.

> *"Suppose there were fifty righteous within the city; would You also destroy the place and not spare it for the fifty righteous that were in it? Far be it from You to do such a thing as this, to slay the righteous with the wicked, so that the righteous should be as the wicked; far be it from You! Shall not the Judge of all the earth do right?"*
>
> *So the Lord said, "If I find in Sodom fifty righteous within the city, then I will spare all the place for their sakes."*

For 50 righteous God agreed to spare all. As the friend of God, Abraham was brokering a deal with the Lord for mercy. Genesis 18:32 shows he continued until God agreed to do this for ten righteous:

> *Then he said, "Let not the Lord be angry, and I will speak but once more: Suppose ten should be found there?"*
>
> *And He said, "I will not destroy it for the sake of ten."*

What an amazing thing that God would allow a man to stand before Him and make decisions concerning the destiny of a people. Yet this is what God actually created man for in the beginning. Genesis 1:26-28 shows us that God's original intent for Adam and Eve was for them to rule and govern the earth with Him.

> *Then God said, "Let Us make man in Our image, according to Our likeness; let them have dominion over the fish of the sea, over the birds of the air, and over the cattle, over all the earth and over every creeping thing that creeps on the earth." So God created man in His own image; in the image of God He created him; male and female He created them. Then God blessed them, and God said to them, "Be fruitful and multiply; fill the earth and subdue it; have dominion over the fish of the sea, over the birds of the air, and over every living thing that moves on the earth."*

The Lord's heart has always been to partner with us to rule the earth. God and us together are to govern the earth until it is a reflection of His kingdom. Adam and Eve together with God were to increase the Garden of Eden through governmental activity until it spread to cover the whole of the earth. All the earth was to have been a reflection of paradise or the kingdom of God in the earth. Man being in the likeness and image of God would have the heart and desires necessary to function in this capacity. God allows us to stand with Him in agreement and be a part of the decision-making process concerning issues in the earth. The more we become in His image and likeness, the more we can be trusted as His friends to be a part of this process.

The word *image* in the Hebrew is *tselem,* and it means a shade. It's the idea of something casting a shadow. As those God has formed, we are to be the *shadow* He is casting. The more we allow ourselves to be fashioned by Him, the more we become a reflection of Him. The word *likeness* is the Hebrew word *dmuwth.* It means to be a model or to resemble. As those created by Him, we are to carry the family resemblance. Those who see us are supposed to encounter Him. As this formation happens in our lives through time spent with the Lord in His presence, we become those qualified to rule the earth together with the Lord. We become His friends who with God can make decisions concerning events, happenings, and futures in the earth. As we stand in the dimension of the spirit called the Council of the Lord, we are allowed the privilege of being a part of this process. What an amazing honor this is.

A fourth thing that is done from this realm called the Council of God is decrees can be made. First Kings 17:1 shows Elijah as a prophet/friend of God operating in this.

> *And Elijah the Tishbite, of the inhabitants of Gilead, said to Ahab, "As the Lord God of Israel lives, before whom I stand, there shall not be dew nor rain these years, except at my word."*

Before I understood the Council of God and its significance, I looked at this scripture differently than I do now. Previously I thought that Elijah had been in a place of prayer and had heard God speak about Ahab. I believed he had then gone to where Ahab was and had proclaimed what he had heard God say. This is not what I understand now. If we read this scripture closely, we see that Elijah declares *"As the Lord God of Israel lives, before whom I stand."* He doesn't say *"before whom I stood."* He says, *"before whom I stand,"* signifying present tense or in the now. Elijah was saying to Ahab, "As I stand here before you in the natural, I am simultaneously standing before the Lord in the spiritual realm. I am standing in two dimensions at one time." From this place that Elijah was standing in the spiritual dimension, he was making a decree of what would be in the natural dimension. He was declaring from the Council of the Lord the reality that would be in the earth. We know this because he says he is *standing* in a place in the spiritual realm. Remember that the Scripture clearly speaks that we *stand* in the Council of the Lord (see Jer. 23:18). As the friend of God, Elijah was granted a place in the Council of God and he decrees from this Council. What he decrees from this place alters what will be in the earth.

Many who are reading this will realize there has been much teaching on decrees connected to prayer. Prayers are not just petitions that we offer. There is a place of authority in God where we can make decrees that cause events to be changed. In other words, we utter words of faith into a spiritual realm that will change things in the natural dimensions. This is what Jesus meant when He spoke about speaking to mountains in Matthew 17:20.

> *So Jesus said to them, "Because of your unbelief; for assuredly, I say to you, if you have faith as a mustard seed, you will say to this mountain, 'Move from here to there,' and it will move; and nothing will be impossible for you."*

Jesus didn't say we would ask God to move the mountain. He said we would speak and the mountain would move. The mountain is symbolic of anything standing in the way of our success, God's purposes, or anything resisting our call in God. Jesus said we would *speak* and the mountain would *move*. Many of us have done the speaking or decreeing, but it seems the mountains haven't budged. What is the problem? I believe it is where we are doing it from in the spiritual realm. We have spoken to the mountains but not from the Council of the Lord. Where we speak and decree *from* is very important to the process. When Elijah spoke from the Council of the Lord, what he said happened. He declared it wouldn't rain until he said it could. Wow! This is exactly what happened. A man standing in the dimension of the spirit called the Council of God as the friend of God decreed a thing and it happened. This is what is promised in the book of Job. Job 22:27-28 tells us the power of living righteously with the Lord.

> *You will make your prayer to Him,*
>
> *He will hear you,*
>
> *And you will pay your vows.*
>
> *You will also declare a thing,*
>
> *And it will be established for you;*
>
> *So light will shine on your ways.*

Through decrees made from the Council of the Lord we can determine what will be in the earth. This is the power of this place in the spirit realm. Words spoken outside this realm may change nothing. Words spoke from this realm can change everything. We can declare a thing and it will be established.

A final thing I will mention that happens in the Council of God is that assignments are given. Isaiah 6:1-9 shows Isaiah standing in the Council of the Lord as the prophet/friend of God.

In the year that King Uzziah died, I saw the Lord sitting on a throne, high and lifted up, and the train of His robe filled the temple. Above it stood seraphim; each one had six wings: with two he covered his face, with two he covered his feet, and with two he flew. And one cried to another and said:

"Holy, holy, holy is the Lord of hosts;

The whole earth is full of His glory!"

And the posts of the door were shaken by the voice of him who cried out, and the house was filled with smoke. So I said:

"Woe is me, for I am undone!

Because I am a man of unclean lips,

And I dwell in the midst of a people of unclean lips;

For my eyes have seen the King,

The Lord of hosts."

Then one of the seraphim flew to me, having in his hand a live coal which he had taken with the tongs from the altar. And he touched my mouth with it, and said:

"Behold, this has touched your lips;

Your iniquity is taken away,

And your sin purged."

Also I heard the voice of the Lord, saying:

"Whom shall I send,

And who will go for Us?"

Then I said, "Here am I! Send me."

And He said, "Go, and tell this people:

'Keep on hearing, but do not understand;

Keep on seeing, but do not perceive.'"

Standing in the Council of the Lord, Isaiah is cleansed by the Lord to another level. In this holy place, Isaiah becomes aware of an uncleanness that is clinging to him. He cries out in repentance. We must be aware that in the Council of God things become manifest for the purpose of cleansing. This can be one of the signs that we are standing in this place of the Spirit. We become aware of any filthiness clinging to us. What didn't bother us outside this realm becomes a problem to us inside this realm. As Isaiah cries out, a heavenly creature flies and takes a coal from the altar of heaven. He touches Isaiah's lips and declares him purged. At this point Isaiah hears the Lord asking, "Who will go for Us?" This is a sure sign that Isaiah is standing in the Council of God. The Lord is asking the Godhead of the Father, Son, and Holy Spirit and/or other beings in this scenario who can take on this assignment. Who will be able to run with the message necessary to God's purpose in the earth? God is asking for counsel in this setting. Isaiah standing in this holy place volunteers for the assignment. He is chosen and given the message he is to run with. In the Council of God people are chosen for assignments and their message is given them.

This has happened in the history of the church. Certain messages that shaped or reshaped the church were given to certain people. John the Baptist came with the message of repentance. This prepared the way for Jesus. Paul was given the message of justification by faith. This altered the way people saw salvation. Martin Luther later would reiterate this message as a spokesman of God. Kenneth Hagin came with the faith message that has had a great influence in the church today. Oral Roberts came with healing. I believe people were chosen from the Council of God and given messages to steward in the church. Others picked them up and began to run with them as well. This caused them to spread. However, they were initially committed to one who would steward them into influence and bring a new dimension to the church.

I personally believe a decision was made that I was to steward the *Courts of Heaven* message in the church. I don't say this arrogantly but based on what I sense and feel, plus what has been prophetically declared to me by others. In the Council of the Lord a decision was made that I was chosen to carry the message of the *Courts of Heaven* and impregnate the Body of Christ with this truth. I have tried to do this diligently as well as keep the excesses out of it that invariably come to new emphasis in the church. I simply say this to make a point that people are chosen and assignments are given in the Council of the Lord.

Notice that in Isaiah's situation he hears this conversation occurring in the Council. He is moved to volunteer in this place. In the Council of the Lord we can be in a dimension where we can volunteer. In fact, in this place you will be moved to volunteer for things that outside this place you would never have wanted to agree to. This is because in this place there is a grace on you for the assignment heaven desires you to carry. Under this grace, you will do things you might never agree to outside it. The fact is that when we agree and say yes to the passion of God in the Council of God, grace will be on us for that assignment. This is what has happened with me. I carry a grace for the assignment I agreed to in His Council. I don't do it from my own strength or inspiration. I do it from the grace I received from the Council of the Lord.

The Council of the Lord is a very powerful dimension of the spirit. In and from this dimension, life on the planet can be changed and shifted into God's will. The Lord needs us to come before Him as His friend and stand in His Council. Like Abraham and Moses of old, we can be a part of determining even the course of nations. What an awesome place to move with God and see His passion fulfilled in the earth. May we receive grace to serve Him acceptably in these realms (see Heb. 12:28).

CHAPTER 8

APPROACHING GOD AS JUDGE

As Jesus continued to teach on prayer in the book of Luke, He introduced the idea of coming before God as the Judge. As we saw that approaching God as Father brings us into the secret place and approaching Him as Friend opens the Council of the Lord, coming before Him as Judge gives us access into the Courts of Heaven. Before we can understand the dimension referred to as the Courts of Heaven, we must know how to come before God as Judge. Many people are comfortable seeing God as Father. Most would be good with seeing God as Friend. Approaching God as Judge, however, might be a little more challenging. This is only because we don't understand the power of this place that works on our behalf. Again, in Luke 18:1-8 we see Jesus putting prayer in a judicial setting.

> *Then He spoke a parable to them, that men always ought to pray and not lose heart, saying: "There was in a certain city a judge who did not fear God nor regard man. Now there was a widow in that city; and she came to him, saying, 'Get justice for me from my adversary.' And he would not for a while; but afterward he said within himself, 'Though I do not fear God nor regard man, yet because this widow troubles me I will avenge her, lest by her continual coming she weary me.'"*
>
> *Then the Lord said, "Hear what the unjust judge said. And shall God not avenge His own elect who cry out day and night to Him, though He bears long with them? I tell you that He will avenge them speedily. Nevertheless, when the Son of Man comes, will He really find faith on the earth?"*

The main message in this story is that if this widow woman with no power, influence, wealth, or might could, through a persistent presentation of her case, get a verdict from a corrupt and unjust judge, how much more will God, the Judge of all, render verdicts and decisions on behalf of His elect! Having said this, we need to understand that coming into the sphere called the Courts of Heaven requires us to approach God as Judge. Just like with the other dimensions of the secret place and the Council of the Lord, the Courts of Heaven have a protocol that must be observed. Just like in a natural court there are protocols that govern them, so it is in the Courts of Heaven.

One of the main protocols is the reverence and honor for the Judge. In the judicial system of the United States, where I reside, when a judge enters the court *all* are expected to rise in honor of the judge's presence. The person and position of judge are to be held in high esteem. If this is true in a natural court, then how much more in the heavenly court where God is the Judge. When approaching God as Judge we must always do so with a humility and surrender before Him. Hebrews 12:23 tells us that we have come to God, the Judge of all.

> *To the general assembly and church of the firstborn who are registered in heaven, to God the Judge of all, to the spirits of just men made perfect.*

As New Testament believers we have been repositioned before God as the Judge of all. This means, as Hebrews 4:12-13 tells us, nothing is hidden from Him and ultimately everything will be judged, unveiled, and seen by Him.

> *For the word of God is living and powerful, and sharper than any two-edged sword, piercing even to the division of soul and spirit, and of joints and marrow, and is a discerner of the thoughts and intents of the heart. And there is no creature hidden from His sight, but all things are naked and open to the eyes of Him to whom we must give account.*

God, as Judge discerns our thoughts and intents. We may fool man, but God is looking at the heart. Just like in the days when God chose David over his brothers to be king of Israel, God looked at the heart. Samuel almost made a mistake in choosing David's oldest brother because of what he looked like in the natural. God quickly spoke to him and changed his mind in First Samuel 16:6-7.

> *So it was, when they came, that he looked at Eliab and said, "Surely the Lord's anointed is before Him!"*

But the Lord said to Samuel, "Do not look at his appearance or at his physical stature, because I have refused him. For the Lord does not see as man sees; for man looks at the outward appearance, but the Lord looks at the heart."

God was not judging from what the natural eye could see. He was discerning the thoughts and intents of the heart. When we come before God as Judge, we must be willing to allow Him to judge us. This means we give Him the right to expose our heart and bring any wrong motives to light. My experience before God as Judge in the Courts of Heaven causes me to believe that in this place things are exposed and revealed. This is a good thing. First Corinthians 11:32 tells us that God corrects us so that He will not have to judge us with the world.

But when we are judged, we are chastened by the Lord,
that we may not be condemned with the world.

So right now, the Lord is disciplining us to remove issues from our hearts so we will not partake of the condemnation that will come on those who are in the world. What a powerful statement. The judgment of God in dealing with us is actually His mercy at work on our behalf. He is judging us now so we will not be judged later and in eternity. This is why we must allow the judging of God to take place in us presently. He is freeing us from things that would require His judgment later. Some of this goes against the grain of what is being taught today in the church. We are told quite often that everything is automatically covered by the blood of Jesus. However, it seems that the blood only speaks for that which is repented of. Hebrews 12:24 tells us the blood of Jesus is speaking on our behalf before the Courts of Heaven. It is giving testimony there.

into. Remember it is through the *reason of use* that these senses are developed. This means we learn to use them by using them. This requires a step of faith as we endeavor to function in the unseen realms. This can be scary and uncertain, but it is necessary to us functioning in these realms of the Spirit. In the next chapter we will talk about the necessity of faith for living in the two worlds of the seen and unseen.

SPIRITUAL SIGHT

Allow me to shed some biblical light on these senses of the Spirit that allow us to function in the unseen realm. We see examples of these prophetic abilities operating in Scripture. For instance, we see Jesus operating with a *seeing* ability in Scripture. When Nathanael came to Jesus, Jesus amazed him by telling him where He *saw* him before he arrived. John 1:47-51 gives a portion of the story.

> *Jesus saw Nathanael coming toward Him, and said of him, "Behold, an Israelite indeed, in whom is no deceit!"*
>
> *Nathanael said to Him, "How do You know me?"*
>
> *Jesus answered and said to him, "Before Philip called you, when you were under the fig tree, I saw you."*
>
> *Nathanael answered and said to Him, "Rabbi, You are the Son of God! You are the King of Israel!"*
>
> *Jesus answered and said to him, "Because I said to you, 'I saw you under the fig tree,' do you believe? You will see greater things than these." And He said to him, "Most assuredly, I say to you, hereafter you shall see heaven open, and the angels of God ascending and descending upon the Son of Man."*

Jesus, through His *sight* in the Spirit, *saw* Nathanael under the fig tree. This astonished Nathanael. He wasn't used to the supernatural realm. As a result of this, Nathanael declared Jesus to be the Son of God. He was very quick to believe and perceive. The reason for this is found in Jesus' statement to him. Jesus said he was *an Israelite indeed in whom there is no deceit.* Nathanael's ability to perceive who Jesus was so quickly was related to his purity of heart. What Jesus said of Nathanael was a reference to Jacob being named Israel after he wrestled all night with an angel. We find this account in Genesis 32:27-28.

> *So He said to him, "What is your name?"*
> *He said, "Jacob."*
> *And He said, "Your name shall no longer be called Jacob, but Israel; for you have struggled with God and with men, and have prevailed."*

The name *Jacob* meant to be crooked and perverse. It meant to deceive. This had been Jacob's nature—to try and get something for himself. God changed his name to *Israel*, which means prince of God and one who has power with God and man. This occurred as Jacob wrestled with God. God touched the hollow of Jacob's thigh and weakened him so he could be subdued. In this weak subdued place, God changed his name.

We all have to go through the wrestlings with God. Through this process we surrender and are subdued under the Lord's gracious authority and power. The result is a change of who we are. The true identity of who we were made to be, even what is written in our book in heaven, can now be revealed. Colossians 3:1-4 tells us that we are to set our desire and affections on the unseen realm above, because that is where our *life* is.

To Jesus the Mediator of the new covenant, and to the blood of sprinkling that speaks better things than that of Abel.

When the Bible speaks of the blood of sprinkling speaking better things than that of Abel, it is speaking of the blood of Abel spilled when his brother Cain killed him. Genesis 4:9-12 shows us the verdict God rendered against Cain because of the murder of his brother Abel.

Then the Lord said to Cain, "Where is Abel your brother?"

He said, "I do not know. Am I my brother's keeper?"

And He said, "What have you done? The voice of your brother's blood cries out to Me from the ground. So now you are cursed from the earth, which has opened its mouth to receive your brother's blood from your hand. When you till the ground, it shall no longer yield its strength to you. A fugitive and a vagabond you shall be on the earth."

The testimony of Abel's blood caused God to sentence Cain to a life of a fugitive and a vagabond. Abel's blood clearly cried for judgment. The blood of Jesus, however, is crying for mercy. This is why the Scripture says Jesus' blood of sprinkling is speaking *better things*. If Jesus had spoken judgment against us, we would have been sealed in our sin. However, He spoke forgiveness and mercy. Luke 23:33-34 shows Jesus asking the Father for mercy and forgiveness for those who were crucifying Him. This is the voice of His blood even now speaking for us.

And when they had come to the place called Calvary, there they crucified Him, and the criminals, one on the

*right hand and the other on the left. Then Jesus said,
"Father, forgive them, for they do not know what they
do."*

And they divided His garments and cast lots.

This epitomizes the heart and cry of Jesus and His blood for us.
He didn't want us judged for our sins. He desired us cleansed and
forgiven of them. There had to be something that would speak for
us before Him. That is His blood of sprinkling. His blood grants
God as Judge the right He needs to forgive us. The judicial system of
heaven demands there be evidence that allows God to forgive. God's
heart is to forgive, but there must be testimony that permits it. It is
the blood of Jesus speaking for us that allows this. Even in the Old
Testament there had to be blood giving testimony for God to roll sin
off the people a year at a time. Every year this had to be redone on the
day of Atonement. Hebrews 10:1-4 reveals that every year the High
Priest would go behind the veil in the temple and offer a sacrifice of
blood for the nation.

> *For the law, having a shadow of the good things to come,
> and not the very image of the things, can never with these
> same sacrifices, which they offer continually year by year,
> make those who approach perfect. For then would they
> not have ceased to be offered? For the worshipers, once
> purified, would have had no more consciousness of sins.
> But in those sacrifices there is a reminder of sins every
> year. For it is not possible that the blood of bulls and
> goats could take away sins.*

The blood of bulls and goats could never *take away sins.* They
could only roll the punishment off for a year. The testimony of the
blood of bulls and goats was only able to bring about this limited

redemption. However, Jesus died and took His own blood and put it on the mercy seat in heaven, and what it is speaking allows us to be completely and totally forgiven. Our sins are not just rolled away for a year; they are completely extracted from us forever, never to be remember again. In fact, they are so removed that their effect against us is demolished. The *voice* of our sin speaking against us is so silenced by the *voice* of His blood that our conscience is cleansed and purified. This is the whole *sprinkling* issue. Hebrews 10:22 tells us what the sprinkling of the blood of Jesus does.

> *Let us draw near with a true heart in full assurance of faith, having our hearts sprinkled from an evil conscience and our bodies washed with pure water.*

When our evil conscience is sprinkled with the blood of the covenant, we can draw near with a true heart in full assurance of being accepted without guilt. Our conscience is no longer condemning us. The sprinkling of the blood is now speaking for us, silencing the voice of our previously evil conscience. We now have complete faith, hope, and assurance of being accepted by Him. We are a new creation because the blood of Jesus is speaking for us and silencing every other voice!

However, the voice of the blood of Jesus only works for us when we come into agreement with it through repentance. Our *confession* brings agreeing testimony before the Courts of Heaven and grants God as Judge the legal right to forgive us. First John 1:9 tells us that *if we confess*, forgiveness and cleansing are secured.

> *If we confess our sins, He is faithful and just to forgive us our sins and to cleanse us from all unrighteousness.*

The word *confess* is the Greek word *homologeo*. It can mean to agree with another's statements and to concede guilt before a judge.

So when we confess, we are agreeing with the conviction of the Holy Spirit. We are agreeing with heaven about us. We are agreeing with the testimony of the blood of Jesus. When we do this according to the Word of God, we are forgiven. My agreement through confession grants me access into what the blood of Jesus says about me. I am now legally forgiven because of my agreement with His blood.

Notice that when we *confess,* we are not just forgiven. We are also cleansed from all unrighteousness. Being forgiven is a legal issue. Cleansing is the power of the Holy Spirit washing away every defilement my sin would have left in my spirit. When I *confess* and concede my guilt, I grant the blood the right to forgive me because of its testimony on my behalf. I also grant the Holy Spirit the right to reach deep in my heart and purify every defiled place. This makes me functionally a new creation. My conscience is cleansed and I am free. My confession allows God as Judge to declare me justified and innocent. All condemnation, guilt, and shame are removed from me. Heaven's Judge and court have rendered me forgiven and cleansed on the basis of Jesus' blood and what it is saying on my behalf!

There are several places in Scripture where we see God spoken of as Judge. We should look at them and gain some insight into what it means to approach Him in this capacity. First Peter 2:21-23 shows how Jesus understood that God was a righteous Judge.

> *For to this you were called, because Christ also suffered*
> *for us, leaving us an example, that you should follow His*
> *steps:*
>
> *"Who committed no sin,*
>
> *Nor was deceit found in His mouth";*

who, when He was reviled, did not revile in return; when He suffered, He did not threaten, but committed Himself to Him who judges righteously.

How could Jesus go through the torment, agony, and suffering He endured without rising to defend Himself? The answer is found in His revelation and understanding of God as the Judge who judges righteously. His power to not strike back was found in the righteous judgments of His Father as the Judge. When we know God as Judge, we can trust in His correct judgments. We know that before it is over, there will be justice because of who our Judge is. If we could just get this in our spirits, it would make us less reactive. We would have a trust and a confidence that cannot be shaken. As a result of Jesus committing Himself to the One who judges righteously, He was raised from the dead, given a better Name than all other names, and is seated at the right hand of God in the highest place. God is just and rewarded Him immensely for His confidence in His righteous judgments. May we too have this revelation of God as the righteous Judge of all the earth. We see this same awareness reflected in Revelation 13:10.

He who leads into captivity shall go into captivity; he who kills with the sword must be killed with the sword. Here is the patience and the faith of the saints.

The confidence that those who hurt and wound will be repaid with the same is the faith and patience of the saints. In other words, the saints believe there is justice with God; therefore, it births the power to endure in them. Knowing God is just and will right all wrongs gives the saints strength and encouragement to continue. When we have this revelation of God as judge, it births this hope in us. Second Thessalonians 1:3-9 gives us a view of the way the early Christians thought in the midst of their persecution and troubles.

We are bound to thank God always for you, brethren, as it is fitting, because your faith grows exceedingly, and the love of every one of you all abounds toward each other, so that we ourselves boast of you among the churches of God for your patience and faith in all your persecutions and tribulations that you endure, which is manifest evidence of the righteous judgment of God, that you may be counted worthy of the kingdom of God, for which you also suffer; since it is a righteous thing with God to repay with tribulation those who trouble you, and to give you who are troubled rest with us when the Lord Jesus is revealed from heaven with His mighty angels, in flaming fire taking vengeance on those who do not know God, and on those who do not obey the gospel of our Lord Jesus Christ. These shall be punished with everlasting destruction from the presence of the Lord and from the glory of His power.

Sometimes we think that as believers we should always be loving, caring, and not wishing hurt on anyone. I will admit this is a fine line to walk. However, in these scriptures the apostle Paul declares that the awareness of God as the righteous Judge, who repays with tribulation those who trouble you, is the hope of those counted worthy of the kingdom of God. He even says the trouble they are experiencing is the evidence of the righteous judgment of God. The idea is that God is allowing it so He can righteously judge those who stand against them and Him. This scripture says that God as the righteous Judge will repay with tribulation those who trouble us while giving us rest! The problem is waiting for the judgment of God during the process. Also, we must keep our hearts free of anger, bitterness, and even vengeance. God is clear that as Judge vengeance belongs to Him. Romans 12:19 tells us that God as Judge reserves the right for vengeance.

Beloved, do not avenge yourselves, but rather give place to wrath; for it is written, "Vengeance is Mine, I will repay," says the Lord.

So when we are waiting on the righteous judgment of God, we must labor to keep our hearts pure. God as Judge will be faithful to judge righteously, but we must leave it completely to Him. This requires grace to work this kind of heart into us and wait for Him as Judge to prevail. Proverbs 24:17-18 actually says that if I allow myself to rejoice when my enemy comes under the judging hand of God, it can cause God to lift the judgement off him.

Do not rejoice when your enemy falls,

And do not let your heart be glad when he stumbles;

Lest the Lord see it, and it displease Him,

And He turn away His wrath from him.

A wrong heart in me can stop the process of God. I must always labor to have a right heart, yet know there is righteous judgement with God as the Judge. When I understand this aspect of God as Judge, I must always follow the leading of the Holy Spirit as I stand before Him. The Holy Spirit will help me to know how to posture myself in agreement with the protocols of the Courts of Heaven.

We also see God revealed as Judge in James 5:1-11. In these scriptures we see rich people oppressing rather than blessing with their riches.

Come now, you rich, weep and howl for your miseries that are coming upon you! Your riches are corrupted, and your garments are moth- eaten. Your gold and silver are corroded, and their corrosion will be a witness against you and will eat your flesh like fire. You have heaped up treasure in the last days. Indeed the wages of the laborers who mowed your fields, which you kept back by fraud, cry out; and the cries of the reapers have reached the ears of the Lord of Sabaoth. You have lived on the earth in pleasure and luxury; you have fattened your hearts as in a day of slaughter. You have condemned, you have murdered the just; he does not resist you.

Therefore be patient, brethren, until the coming of the Lord. See how the farmer waits for the precious fruit of the earth, waiting patiently for it until it receives the early and latter rain. You also be patient. Establish your hearts, for the coming of the Lord is at hand.

Do not grumble against one another, brethren, lest you be condemned. Behold, the Judge is standing at the door! My brethren, take the prophets, who spoke in the name of the Lord, as an example of suffering and patience. Indeed we count them blessed who endure. You have heard of the perseverance of Job and seen the end intended by the Lord—that the Lord is very compassionate and merciful.

This passage of Scripture is revealing God as Judge with regard to people not receiving what is rightfully theirs for their labors. Notice that their riches and the corrosion of them will be a *witness* against those who hold back the wages. This is the Greek word *marturion*. It means something evidential. It means to testify and give a testimony. It is something that happens in a judicial system. So the Scripture is saying that money gives testimony in the spirit realm, which allows God as Judge to render judgment against oppressive economic systems. Systems that hold people in the bondage of poverty, God will judge when the cry of the laborers agrees with the cry of the money held back. God promises to bring justice into these situations.

We are then exhorted to not grumble against others, because *the Judge* is standing at the door. This would seem to imply that judgement is near. Clearly our complaining and speaking evil of others is of consequence before God as Judge. We must be very careful of the things that come from our lips against others. Our words can work against us when the Judge is hearing them and aware of them. James then begins to speak of the justice of God seen in the occasion of Job. Job lost everything because the devil brought a *court case* against him. In the *end,* however, Job was rewarded and restored with double everything he lost. This was the justice of God rendered in Job's life from God the Judge of all the earth. It is interesting that before God rendered the verdict of double restoration, Job had to pray for his friends who had not stood with him in his afflictions. Job 42:10 tells us that Job found restoration when he prayed for the friends of his who had not helped him during his troubles.

> *And the Lord restored Job's losses when he prayed for his friends. Indeed the Lord gave Job twice as much as he had before.*

This scripture is very clear. When Job prayed for these faithless, false-counseling friends, God gave Job twice everything he had lost. There was something about Job's gracious attitude that allowed God as Judge to render his restitution on his behalf. If we are to see God as Judge move for us, we must guard our mouth and also walk in a spirit of forgiveness toward those who might have hurt and offended us. This obviously has great power before God as Judge. It allows Him to render decisions for us from His courts.

Rachel also understood the power of God as Judge working for her. Genesis 30:6 shows Rachel crediting the ability to give birth to children after years of barrenness to God as Judge deciding in her favor.

> *Then Rachel said, "God has judged my case; and He has*
> *also heard my voice and given me a son." Therefore she*
> *called his name Dan.*

Rachel desperately desired to have children with Jacob. However, her womb was shut up. She was forced to sit by and watch her sister Leah and their handmaidens have children. The pain of this as they rejoiced must have been unbearable as she sat in her barrenness. She clearly had cried out to God. The miraculous occurred. Her hand-maiden gave birth to Dan. Her declaration was "God has judged my case." She had been presenting her petitions and case before the Judge of the earth and had found favor in His eyes. He came to remove her pain. It's interesting that she named this son Dan. Dan means *judge*. Genesis 49:16 actually shows the tribes being prophesied over. Dan is declared to be a judge.

> *Dan shall judge his people*
> *As one of the tribes of Israel.*

Out of Rachel's pain and her cry before God as Judge, God raised up a judge to administer righteousness and justice. From Rachel's revelation of God as a Judge who would hear her case, God produced a judge who would represent Him in the earth. Rachel had presented her case to the ultimate Judge and had found favor in His eyes. Her voice was heard and God had granted her request. Her years of frustration and pain were over. How often do we go through pain and frustration but don't know where to go with it? We must be as Rachel and take it before the Judge and let Him hear our voice. We must know how to present our case in His courts and see Him render decisions and verdicts on our behalf. Not only did Rachel's handmaiden give birth to Dan, Rachel herself would later give birth to Joseph from her opened womb. Joseph would be the preserver of life who would save nations from extinction, including the budding nation of Israel. Genesis 45:5 shows Joseph being aware of His reason and destiny.

> *But now, do not therefore be grieved or angry with your-*
> *selves because you sold me here; for God sent me before*
> *you to preserve life.*

Through the cry of Rachel to God as Judge, the one who would be used to preserve life in the nations was rightly positioned. The emptiness, pain, and years of misery endured by Rachel were not for nothing. They brought her to a place of presenting her case before God the Judge and Him rendering a verdict on her behalf. Please know that regardless of what we are going through, there is a Judge who judges righteously. He is awaiting our petition before Him to render decisions for us. He takes into account the pain we have endured even unrighteously when deciding for us. I have come to real-ize that any mistreatment, abuse, and/or hurt I might have endured actually works for my benefit before the Judge of heaven and earth. Again, this is what we see in the abuse and torture of Jesus as our Savior. First Peter 2:21-23 shows us that Jesus' power to endure this inhuman pain was the fact He was convinced God as Judge would reward Him for it.

> *For to this you were called, because Christ also suffered*
> *for us, leaving us an example, that you should follow His*
> *steps:*
> *"Who committed no sin,*
> *Nor was deceit found in His mouth";*

who, when He was reviled, did not revile in return;
when He suffered, He did not threaten, but committed
Himself to Him who judges righteously.

Jesus was absolutely confident that the torment of His abusers
would be recompensed by the decisions of God His Father as the
Judge. The Bible actually speaks of suffering and afflictions having
this effect before God on our behalf. Colossians 1:24 reveals Paul's
awareness of what his suffering was accomplishing.

I now rejoice in my sufferings for you, and fill up in my
flesh what is lacking in the afflictions of Christ, for the
sake of His body, which is the church.

Paul understood that his hardships and persecutions were *filling*
up something in the spirit realm that would allow God the right to
render judgments. Jesus spoke of this in Matthew 23:31-32.

Therefore you are witnesses against yourselves that you
are sons of those who murdered the prophets. Fill up,
then, the measure of your fathers' guilt.

In speaking to the religious leaders of His day, Jesus said they
were actually releasing testimony against themselves by claiming
their lineage. They were acknowledging that their fathers had killed
the prophets and they were therefore worthy of judgment. Jesus proclaims, "Fill up, then, the measure of your fathers' guilt." In other
words, He is saying, *"Through your activities and resistance to Me and*
My words, you give the legal right for judgment to come on you as a hard-
ened nation." This is exactly what happened to Israel. It was because
they *filled up* something in the spirit realm that demanded judgment
from God as Judge. The same thing can be true of us. When we have
suffered before the Lord, that suffering speaks on our behalf and *fills*
up what is necessary for God to relieve and even bless us. First Peter

3:8-9 declares we must go against our natural inclination to speak evil and curse in the midst of being harmed.

> *Finally, all of you be of one mind, having compassion for one another; love as brothers, be tenderhearted, be courteous; not returning evil for evil or reviling for reviling, but on the contrary blessing, knowing that you were called to this, that you may inherit a blessing.*

When we are confident of our future and our destiny, we can speak blessings even in the midst of harmful and hurtful things. The Judge who is in heaven is watching. He is evaluating everything that would speak concerning us. Notice that Peter in this scripture connects suffering to inheriting a blessing. So when we suffer and are mistreated, it is testimony that speaks for us in heaven that brings a judgment forth on our behalf. God is moved to release our inherited blessing to us because of the suffering we have endured!

I have experienced this very thing. Mary and I have gone through persecution, thievery, character assault and assassination, loss, and much pain. I'm not saying others haven't known this as well; I'm just recounting our life. In the midst of this, we have *tried* to walk in the fear of the Lord and maintain a right heart before the Lord. We have sought to have a soft and pliable heart before His presence. After many years of rejection, lies, and even abuse, I had a dream. In my dream, one from the Cloud of Witnesses (see Heb. 12:1) began to prophesy over me. As they prophesied over me, someone stood up and interrupted. This one from this spirit dimension then very sternly declared, "It's Robert's turn." I *knew* in the dream they were declaring, "He's been left out, passed over, abused, and mistreated, but heaven has decided it's now his turn." From the point of this dream on, a new favor came over my life. New doors, opportunities, blessings, and prosperity were released to me. This was because God had looked on my afflictions and decided, "Enough is enough." The Judge had rendered a verdict for me! Exodus 4:31 shows the people being aware of God *looking on their affliction* and moving for them because of it.

> *So the people believed; and when they heard that the Lord had visited the children of Israel and that He had looked on their affliction, then they bowed their heads and worshiped.*

God was going to deliver the people from Egyptian rule at this time because God saw their affliction and pain. Pain before the Lord can give a very powerful testimony. It grants God the right as Judge to vindicate us and move concerning us. May God grant us the power and heart to maintain our integrity before Him as we walk through our pain. That I might be found worthy of His deliverance in my life! First Peter 5:10 unveils Peter confirming this principle.

> *But may the God of all grace, who called us to His eternal glory by Christ Jesus, after you have suffered a while, perfect, establish, strengthen, and settle you.*

Notice that *after we have suffered a while* God would perfect, establish, strengthen, and settle us. Why would we have to wait *a while* before God would do this for us? It is our suffering speaking before Him that allows the judgment to be rendered on our behalf. We must walk in a way that allows God as Judge to move for us. May we each have grace to respond in the appropriate way so the decisions of heaven can come for us. God as Judge is waiting for us to come and present ourselves before Him. May great grace be on us all.

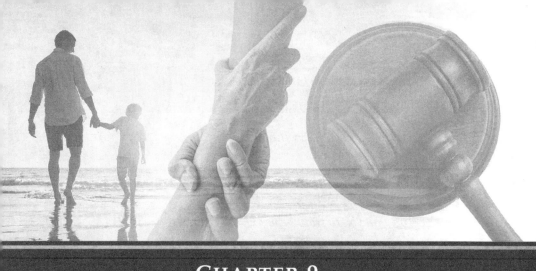

CHAPTER 9

THE COURTS
OF HEAVEN

JUST LIKE APPROACHING GOD AS FATHER AND APPROACHING Him as Friend opens up dimensions of the spirit—the secret place and the Council of the Lord—so approaching God as Judge opens up *the Courts of Heaven*. The Courts of Heaven is not a method of praying. The Courts of Heaven is a spiritual dimension. When we by faith come before God as Judge, we can step into the Courts of Heaven and present ourselves and our cases to the Lord. Daniel 7:9-10 gives us a view of this dimension of the spirit realm that Daniel saw into.

> *I watched till thrones were put in place,*
> *And the Ancient of Days was seated;*

His garment was white as snow,

And the hair of His head was like pure wool.

His throne was a fiery flame,

Its wheels a burning fire;

A fiery stream issued

And came forth from before Him.

A thousand thousands ministered to Him;

Ten thousand times ten thousand stood before Him.

The court was seated,

And the books were opened.

Daniel is *watching* in the spirit realm. He *sees* things set in judicial order in this realm in which he is looking. He *sees* six distinct things happen in this realm that are going to allow verdicts to alter life in the earth. He sees *thrones put into place.* He sees the *Ancient of Days seated on His throne.* He sees *a fiery stream issued.* He sees *thousands upon thousands ministering to Him.* He sees *the court seated.* He sees *the books opened.* All this activity is happening in the spirit realm called the Courts of Heaven. When we step by faith into this dimension, we enter and become a part of this activity. Before we discuss these six things I've mentioned, let me help us be fully aware of our right to function in this place. Hebrews 12:22-24 is a clear depiction of the legal realm of the spirit we have been called to function in.

But you have come to Mount Zion and to the city of the living God, the heavenly Jerusalem, to an innumerable company of angels, to the general assembly and church of the firstborn who are registered in heaven, to God the Judge of all, to the spirits of just men made perfect, to

> *Jesus the Mediator of the new covenant, and to the blood*
> *of sprinkling that speaks better things than that of Abel.*

As I said earlier concerning this scripture, this can relate to both the *Council of the Lord* and the *Court of Heaven* dimensions. These two realms are very closely related, though I believe them to be different. The main difference is there is no adversary in the Council, while there is one to contend with in the Courts. Having said this, this scripture shows us the legal characteristics of what is being described here. For instance, the word *church* is the Greek word *ecclesia*. It speaks of those *called out* for governmental, judicial, and legislative purposes. As the church, we are here to take our place in a legal dimension of the spirit realm. This scripture also speaks of God as the Judge of all. This is the capacity in which He is functioning in this place. The *spirits of just men* is a reference to the *Cloud of Witnesses*. They are those who give judicial testimony. Jesus is occupying this place as the *Mediator of the New Covenant*. These are both legal and judicial terms. Even the *blood that is speaking* is talking about that which is giving judicial testimony.

Clearly this scripture is describing a legal realm of the spirit where we have *come to*. This means that by virtue of Jesus' sacrifice for us, we have been repositioned in the realm of the spirit and now are standing in and have access to this place. We must accept this by faith and begin to present our cases before God as the Judge of all. He is waiting for us to operate in the place He has granted us. Isaiah 43:25-28 gives us further admonishment concerning our operation in this sphere.

> *I, even I, am He who blots out your transgressions for My*
> *own sake;*
>
> *And I will not remember your sins.*

Put Me in remembrance;

Let us contend together;

State your case, that you may be acquitted.

Your first father sinned,

And your mediators have transgressed against Me.

Therefore I will profane the princes of the sanctuary;

I will give Jacob to the curse,

And Israel to reproaches.

Isaiah is urging the people of Israel to state their case. He is letting them know that if they don't take their place before the Courts of Heaven, the destiny of their nation will be lost. They will come under a curse and a reproach. He is pressing them to deal with the legal issues of transgression, their fathers' sin, and any and all things the devil would use to devour them. We too must not neglect this realm of the spirit we have been granted a place in. We must operate in this place *we have come to.* When we do, breakthrough and securing of destiny can be had. As we approach God as Judge, we take up the place we have been granted in this place of the spirit called the Courts of Heaven.

Now to look at the six things that Daniel saw as he *watched* in the spirit realm. This can give us insight into this place that we are standing and accessing by faith. When Daniel speaks of *watching,* he is talking of functioning as a *seer.* My purpose in this book is not to get deeply into this idea. Just suffice it to say that we all have the ability to perceive in the realms of the spirit. As New Testament believers, we can discern prophetically what is happening in the unseen realm. This is why Daniel speaks of *watching.* He is perceiving in the realm of the spirit what is happening. We can do this by *seeing, hearing, feeling, knowing, and otherwise discerning* the activity of the unseen dimension. We all are challenged to continually be developing these abilities. We shouldn't be afraid of this but should rather embrace it and learn progressively to operate there.

THRONES PUT INTO PLACE

The first thing Daniel saw was *thrones being put into place*. This is *not* the throne of God. This is thrones, plural. We know from Revelation 4:4 that there are at least 24 thrones that beings called *elders* sit on.

> *Around the throne were twenty-four thrones, and on the thrones I saw twenty-four elders sitting, clothed in white robes; and they had crowns of gold on their heads.*

These 24 are a part of the judicial operation of heaven. However, I don't think this is what Daniel is referring to. The reason is that the *thrones* Daniel saw were being *put into place*. This means to me that they were not there previously. In other words, something is allowing these thrones to be established as something that is necessary to the Courts of Heaven operation. It would appear to me that the Court of Heaven is more a *tribunal* than what we would think of as a civil court. A tribunal is a court of justice for international war crimes or a seat or bench for judges. So the thrones being set in place were those being positioned as a tribunal or decision-making group in the Courts of Heaven. Who would occupy these thrones being *put* into place?

Those who would sit on these thrones are those who have obtained the right from the lives they have lived and their history in God. Jesus declared in Revelation 3:21 that those who overcome are allowed to *sit* with Him in His throne.

To him who overcomes I will grant to sit with Me on My throne, as I also overcame and sat down with My Father on His throne.

Overcomers are those who are granted a seat in the spirit realm of heavenly activity. These can be people who are already in heaven or they are yet alive in the earth. Just because someone is not dead yet, it doesn't preclude them from this place in the heavenly realm. Remember that we live in two dimensions at one time and are functioning as natural people in a natural world while we are *seated with Him in heavenly places* (see Eph. 2:6). It is very possible to be alive in this earthly realm yet occupy a seat or a throne in the heavenly dimension. In fact, I believe God has to have people who have qualified for this place before His will can be done in the earth. Psalm 115:16 tells us that God gave earth to man.

The heaven, even the heavens, are the Lord's;
But the earth He has given to the children of men.

The Lord must have those who are yet in the earth to partner with Him so that the earth can be impacted. We are the ones with the authority to see His will be done here. When we function in the heavenly realm while yet in the earth, we can grant God the legal rights He needs to see His will done in this place. Because He has given the earth to the children of men, we determine from this authority what will and will not be in the earth. When there are those who sit on the thrones in heavenly places, we can grant God rights that those who are now in heaven cannot grant Him. We must partner with the heavenly arena for God's will to be done in the earth!

So the Courts of Heaven operation depends on *thrones being put into place.* Without these thrones in place and representation from the earth realm in heavenly dimensions, God's passion cannot impact the earth. There must be those who are sitting on thrones in the heavenly Court. I have had several dreams where I saw myself sitting in seats or thrones in the spiritual world. In one dream, I was dusting off and putting back in place a *seat/throne* that had been neglected and not used. I pulled it back into place or put it there and then sat in it. I knew this throne had not had anyone sit in it for a long time. Either no one had qualified or through ignorance it wasn't being occupied. As a result, certain things *could not* happen in the earth.

I believe there are many thrones like this. Through spiritual activity and faith, we must get them back into place and sit in them. The Court of Heaven cannot operate until they are *put into place and occupied.* In another dream I saw a seat vacated because the one who had occupied it had died. When they left the seat, it was disrupted and slightly moved out of order. I went and placed the seat back into right position and sat in it. This tells me in the earthly realm there are seats that become open when people die. It verifies my idea that God needs people in seats in the heavenly realm while they are in the earthly realm. When they transition to heaven these seats become open.

There must be those who can set them in order and take their place in these thrones. God needs judges in the earth realm in seats in the heavenly realm as a part of the Court of Heaven. In the third dream I had about a seat/throne, I saw one hovering in the atmosphere. I was told of things I would need to do that would allow me to sit in this seat. As long as I did what I was told to do, I would have a right to sit in this seat and function from it in the Courts of Heaven. I have endeavored to fulfill the requirements mandated to me to sit in this seat!

The Court of Heaven operation is dependent on thrones being set into place. The tribunal of heaven is waiting for us in earth to agree with heaven and get into our seats as overcomers. When we do, we have helped the Court of Heaven begin to function concerning things in the earth. Through prayer, faith, obedience, and laying our life down to serve the Lord, we can be granted a place to sit in the heavenly dimension. This allows us to be a necessary part of the Court of Heaven operation. Life can change on the earth because we are in our throne or seat in the spiritual dimension.

THE ANCIENT OF DAYS SEATED

A second thing Daniel saw was the *Ancient of Days* taking His place. This is obviously a reference to the Lord Himself. It speaks of His eternal position. He has ruled the earth and will rule it forever. Revelation 1:8 says He is the one who was, is, and is yet to come.

> *"I am the Alpha and the Omega, the Beginning and the End," says the Lord, "who is and who was and who is to come, the Almighty."*

As the Ancient of Days, the Lord is God of the past, the present, and of the future. His activities hold all things together and determine what will be. He is the One sitting on the ultimate Throne. We know who He is from the past, we know who He is in the present, but there is always more to come. He will continue to be revealed to us for all eternity to be.

He is always *yet to come!* He is the One sitting on the Throne of Heaven and rendering judgments concerning the earth.

THE FIERY THRONE OF GOD

Daniel also saw the fiery throne of God and the fiery stream coming from it. This means the Throne of God is full of passion and renders verdicts full of zeal. The throne of God is not a passive place. It is a place where God's judgments are set in place and are fulfilled. Isaiah 9:7 speaks of the zeal of the Lord to establish His kingdom purposes in the earth.

> *Of the increase of His government and peace*
> *There will be no end,*
> *Upon the throne of David and over His kingdom,*
> *To order it and establish it with judgment and justice*
> *From that time forward, even forever.*
> *The zeal of the Lord of hosts will perform this.*

From His Throne of fire, fiery streams or verdicts come forth. In the zeal of God, there is a setting in place that is necessary for His kingdom will to be done. Psalm 97:3 tells us that God sends forth fire and burns up all His enemies that would resist His purpose.

> *A fire goes before Him,*
> *And burns up His enemies round about.*

This is the zeal and fiery streams coming forth from His Throne of fire. When verdicts and decisions are made and released from His Throne, anything that stands against them will perish. Decisions from the Court of Heaven are set in order. Anything that would seek to work against them is consumed. Hebrews 12:28-29 tells us that God in His nature is a consuming fire.

> *Therefore, since we are receiving a kingdom which cannot*
> *be shaken, let us have grace, by which we may serve God*

*acceptably with reverence and godly fear. For our God is
a consuming fire.*

As a result of God being a consuming fire, we are exhorted to cry out for grace to serve Him acceptably. The awareness of God being this consuming fire causes us to recognize our own frailty. We realize our need to be empowered to walk before a holy God whose decisions from His throne are streams of fire. We must have a walk worthy of ones who serve the God who is the Judge of all the earth. May we be filled with His grace to stand before His Courts.

THOUSANDS UPON THOUSANDS MINISTERING

Daniel then sees the *thousands upon thousands* ministering to the One who sits on the Throne. These are the angelic beings but also the myriad of worshipers before Him. We see this in Revelation 5:11-12.

> *Then I looked, and I heard the voice of many angels around the throne, the living creatures, and the elders; and the number of them was ten thousand times ten thousand, and thousands of thousands, saying with a loud voice:*
>
> *"Worthy is the Lamb who was slain*
>
> *To receive power and riches and wisdom,*
>
> *And strength and honor and glory and blessing!"*

All of these heavenly beings are giving glory to the Lamb of God and the One who sits on the Throne. They are part of the worship experience of heaven. As I have said before in other books on the Courts of Heaven, worship creates the atmosphere the Courts of Heaven operate in. If you want to stand in the Courts of Heaven, then engage and be a worshiper. As we worship, we join the multitudes who are worshiping at His Throne. Our worship can touch the One who sits on the Throne and can be a part of decisions being rendered from His Courts.

THE COURT SEATED

The Bible then says Daniel saw the *Court seated*. The Court being seated means it is now ready to proceed and operate. When a Judge comes into a court in my country of the United States, all people rise. The judge then takes his seat and calls the court to order. Everyone is then seated and the court is now ready to hear cases presented. When Daniel sees the *Court seated,* it is declaring the Court of Heaven is now ready to entertain cases and petitions offered to it. The Court is now in session. This is significant because it means this is a time when we can present our cry to God and He will hear. Isaiah 55:6 tells us that we should petition the Lord when He is close to us.

> *Seek the Lord while He may be found,*
> *Call upon Him while He is near.*

This scripture would seem to imply that there is an awareness of when God is ready to hear our prayers. I believe it is important to recognize when the *Court is in session.* Even though I believe God is omnipresent and can always hear our cry, I also believe when we sense an urging of the Spirit to pray, we should follow that leading. It could be that the Court is seated and ready to render verdicts and decisions on our behalf.

THE BOOKS OPENED

The last thing Daniel watched was the books being opened. Of course, I cover this idea in my other books on the Courts of Heaven.

Psalm 139:16 depicts the fact that we all have a book in heaven with our destiny, future, and purpose for existence written in it.

Your eyes saw my substance, being yet unformed. And in Your book they all were written,

The days fashioned for me,

When as yet there were none of them.

When the books are opened, it implies that something is going to be presented from these books into the Courts of Heaven. As we have an awareness of what is written in our books concerning our purpose and destiny, we should present this in the Courts of Heaven. Through prophetic insight, we become aware of the reason we are here. We then began to ask the Lord for the fullness of what is written in our book. Isaiah 43:26 tells us to put God in remembrance.

Put Me in remembrance;

Let us contend together;

State your case, that you may be acquitted.

Putting God in remembrance means reminding Him of what was written in our book in heaven. When we do this, we are presenting cases in the Courts of Heaven. We are asking God as Judge to render decisions on our behalf that we might have what has been written in our book. We present our prophetic destiny as a petition before the Court of Heaven.

These six things Daniel saw as he watched. He was witnessing what was happening in the Courts of Heaven where God sat as Judge. By faith, we too can come and petition this Court. As we approach God as Judge by faith, we come to stand in the Courts and make our case before Him. This allows God as Judge to move on our behalf, grant our desires, and fulfill His passions. We are standing in this realm of the spirit where much heavenly activity is. We may not see it, but we know it is there by faith. We become a part of that which is happening in the spiritual dimension. We stand before God the Judge and see decisions and verdicts rendered at our request.

CHAPTER 10

ANSWERING ACCUSATIONS AND RECEIVING ANSWERS FROM THE COURTS OF HEAVEN

As WE STAND IN THIS SPIRITUAL PLACE CALLED THE Courts of Heaven, we can function there effectively. Revelation 12:10-11 gives us major insight on how to present our cases in this place.

> *Then I heard a loud voice saying in heaven, "Now salvation, and strength, and the kingdom of our God,*

and the power of His Christ have come, for the accuser
of our brethren, who accused them before our God day
and night, has been cast down. And they overcame him
by the blood of the Lamb and by the word of their testi-
mony, and they did not love their lives to the death."

This portion of Scripture unveils for us a judicial activity going on in heaven. The word *accuser* is the Greek word *katagoros*. It means a complainant at law or one who stands against us in the assembly. This means what is being described here is a judicial place in the spirit realm where accusations are being brought against us. However, He still seeks to function from this place, and we must take what Jesus did to silence accusations against us today. This is why the apostle Peter in First Peter 5:8 refers to the devil as a legal agent still seeking legal rights to devour us.

Be sober, be vigilant; because your adversary the devil
walks about like a roaring lion, seeking whom he may
devour.

The Greek word for *adversary* is *antidikos*. It means a legal oppo-nent or one who brings a lawsuit. Peter is declaring here that the devil works from a legal place to seek to devour us. He is warning us that we must be on guard not to grant him this right. Even though Satan has been defeated by Jesus and His atoning work, he is still trying anything legal to gain an advantage over us. We must know how to stand in the Courts of Heaven and deal with these issues. When we do, we get the breakthrough that is ours because of Jesus and what He has done.

The scripture we read in Revelation declares three things neces-sary to win this legal struggle. We are to overcome the accuser by the blood of the Lamb, the word of our testimony, and not loving our life unto death. These three things operated in from the Courts of Heaven allow what God desires for us to become reality. The blood of the Lamb is used to *undo* any and every case against us. Hebrews 12:24 tells us that the blood of Jesus is speaking for us.

> *To Jesus the Mediator of the new covenant, and to the blood of sprinkling that speaks better things than that of Abel.*

THE BLOOD OF THE LAMB

We know the *blood speaking* is a reference to something judicial because Abel's blood gave testimony that caused God to judge Cain. Genesis 4:10-11 shows the blood of Abel crying out and God as a result judging Cain.

> *And He said, "What have you done? The voice of your brother's blood cries out to Me from the ground. So now you are cursed from the earth, which has opened its mouth to receive your brother's blood from your hand."*

The testimony of Abel's blood against Cain caused judgment to come from the heavenly Court against him. There is good news, though. The blood of Jesus is speaking better things on our behalf. The blood of Jesus grants God the legal right to forgive and not judge us. Abel's blood demanded judgement against Cain. However, Jesus' blood cries out for mercy and forgiveness. Regardless of anything speaking against us from the accuser, the blood of the Lamb speaks for us. Because of what Jesus' blood is declaring, God has the legal right to forgive us. We must simply repent and agree with the blood of the Lamb speaking for us from His mercy seat.

THE WORD OF OUR TESTIMONY

The next thing mentioned is the word of our testimony. Of course, *testimony* is a legal reference. The blood revokes any voice against us. The word of our testimony is how we present a case before the Lord. A Court cannot render decisions in our behalf just because an accusation is removed. We also need that which speaks for us. In other words, we need to present our own case. This is the word of our testimony. There are at least five distinct things we can use to present our own case. We first must present our petition based on what is written in our book in heaven (see Ps. 139:16). We have spoken of this earlier. We must prophetically discern what is written in our book through words we have heard, impressions we have felt, desires we recognize, and other means. As we do, we should then present this as a case before the Lord. We bring our prophetic understanding of what is in our book to the Lord. This is presenting our case. The second thing we can do is present any prophetic words we have received. Paul told Timothy in First Timothy 1:18 that he had to war for the prophetic words he had received to become reality.

> *This charge I commit to you, son Timothy, according to the prophecies previously made concerning you, that by them you may wage the good warfare.*

Timothy had to contend for the prophetic destiny to come to pass. Once a prophetic word is spoken to us, the enemy will build a case against us to resist it. We must know how to come before the Lord and undo any case the devil would use to stop the intent of God expressed through this word. This is what Daniel did in Daniel 9:2-5.

> *In the first year of his reign I, Daniel, understood by the books the number of the years specified by the word of*

202

the Lord through Jeremiah the prophet, that He would accomplish seventy years in the desolations of Jerusalem.

Then I set my face toward the Lord God to make request by prayer and supplications, with fasting, sackcloth, and ashes. And I prayed to the Lord my God, and made confession, and said, "O Lord, great and awesome God, who keeps His covenant and mercy with those who love Him, and with those who keep His commandments, we have sinned and committed iniquity, we have done wickedly and rebelled, even by departing from Your precepts and Your judgments."

When Daniel understood the intent of God based on the prophecies of Jeremiah, he began to pray and repent. He was dealing with any legal reason the devil would use to stop the fulfillment of Jeremiah's word. Many prophecies never come to pass, not because they aren't from God but because the enemy uses something legal to stop them. When Daniel repented for himself and the nation, the legal rights of Satan were revoked. There could be an *on-time* fulfillment of that which had been spoken. We too must know how to contend for the prophecies we carry. We should present them to the Lord as a petition in His Courts. When we do, we are making our own case as the word of our testimony.

Another thing we can do to present our own case in the Courts of Heaven is remind God of what Jesus has done. The blood and body of Jesus and His sacrifice speaks for us. As I was praying with a mother over the phone for her 23-year-old daughter to be healed, I became aware that the sacrifice of Jesus was speaking for her. This daughter was in serious condition because of complications after surgery. I heard the Lord declare that His sacrifice was speaking for her before the Courts of Heaven. I knew she would recover and be healed, which she did. When I sensed this, I simply began to agree with what the sacrifice of Jesus was speaking for her. We must know how to present the atoning work of Jesus as evidence of our case before the Lord. This is very powerful in the Courts of Heaven concerning us.

The promises of the Word of God are also that which we can use to present our case before the Lord. There are myriads of promises in God's Word. It is absolutely appropriate to take the promises of the Word of God and remind Him of them in His Courts. When we do this, we are allowing the Word of God to speak as a testimony in our behalf. His Word and God Himself are absolutely the same. Jesus is even called the Word of God. Revelation 19:13 records that Jesus in all His splendor and glory is called the Word of God.

> *He was clothed with a robe dipped in blood, and His name is called The Word of God.*

To deny His Word would be to deny Himself and He will not do this. When we present His Word as testimony in the Courts of Heaven, it is powerful. Second Timothy 2:13 actually declares that even if we are unfaithful God, cannot deny Himself. He will be faithful to His covenant and the promises of His Word.

> *If we are faithless,*
>
> *He remains faithful;*
>
> *He cannot deny Himself.*

We should boldly come before the Courts of Heaven and present the promises of the Word of God as testimony for our breakthrough. God loves it when we take Him at His Word.

Another way we present testimony before the Lord is through our giving. Money and finances have a testimony before the Lord.

Hebrews 7:8 tells us the tithe releases witnesses in the Courts of Heaven.

Here mortal men receive tithes, but there he receives them, of whom it is witnessed that he lives.

When we bring our tithe to the Lord and honor Him, it is releasing a witness that we believe He lives. This means we have access into not only all His death purchased for us, but also all His life grants us. The honoring of the Lord with the tithe releases our legal claims on this in the Courts of Heaven. The money we give actually speaks on our behalf before His Courts. This is what happened with Cornelius and his house in Acts 10:4.

And when he observed him, he was afraid, and said, "What is it, lord?"

So he said to him, "Your prayers and your alms have come up for a memorial before God."

The angel sent to his house informed Cornelius that his giving and his prayers caused God to remember him. When we are tithers, givers, and those who honor the Lord financially, it speaks for us and causes us and our house to be remembered before the Lord. It is a memorial that speaks concerning us and allows God to remember us and render decisions for us. These are just some ways we can release the word of our testimony before the Lord.

NOT LOVING OUR LIFE UNTO DEATH

The other thing mentioned was they loved not their life unto death. In other words when we lay our lives down in sacrifice to the Lord, it grants us a great place of authority to pray from in the Courts of Heaven. This is not only speaking of dying naturally. It is speaking of sacrificing our own desires, longings, and even fleshly impulses to

205

serve the Lord. When we do this, it grants us an authority to pray from in His Courts. Jesus spoke of this in John 10:17.

> *Therefore My Father loves Me, because I lay down My*
> *life that I may take it again.*

The word *life* is the Greek word *psuche*. It means a soulish life. It doesn't just mean the natural life or breath. It can also mean our desires, wants, and choices. In other words, when I lay down what I want and desire for God, Jesus said the Father loves us. This is not about performance or anything of that nature. It is speaking of being granted a place of power and authority before the Lord because we have chosen His ways instead of our own. When the Bible speaks of not loving our lives unto death, it is speaking of this. We are granted the honor of choosing the ways of the Lord. When we do, our prayers will carry new levels of weight in the Courts of Heaven.

As we step into the Courts of Heaven by approaching God as Judge, we can present cases before Him that alter destinies. We can see His will done in the earth and breakthrough come for us and our families. Jesus is faithful and will teach us how to pray, even as He did the first disciples.

CHAPTER 11

ACTIVATE, PARTICIPATE, DEMONSTRATE

W E HAVE SEEN THE THREE REALMS OF PRAYER JESUS taught His disciples. He taught them to approach God as Father, Friend, and Judge. This activity opens spiritual dimensions that we can live in and function from. We can step into the secret place, the Council of the Lord, and the Courts of Heaven. Each of these are very powerful places in the spirit that we can operate in and see breakthrough. The problem is none of this does us any good unless we take the step and try. We can have the information but never gain any advantage from it. We must set aside the time to spend with the Lord in His presence. When we do, these realms will not be just an idea; they will become an experience. So my challenge to you is this. Activate your faith and take practical steps. Set aside time in the morning, at night, or whenever you can carve it out and seek the face of the Lord. This is what I had to do more than 38 years ago. I knew I was to pray. However, I had to actually make it happen. I had to activate my faith and give it a try. It wasn't easy and my flesh didn't want to do it. However, 38 years later, I am so very grateful that I did. It changed me. It changed my family. It made me who I am today. All because I chose to activate what I understood the Lord desired.

The second thing is to participate. I was not blessed initially to be able to pray with others. I had to do it by myself. However, praying with others of like mind and heart can be very beneficial. You can draw from the faith and prophetic understanding of each other.

I usually tell people one of the best ways to learn to pray is to pray with those who know how. Having said this, most prayer meeting I know are dry, boring, and powerless. I am not speaking of these gatherings when I exhort you to participate. The prayer meetings I speak of are with those who host and cultivate the presence of the Lord. Everything they do flows from His presence. When prayer meetings are done right, they can be the most powerful place of encountering His presence you can find. Out of this place of glory, things begin to shift into the divine order of God. One of the greatest compliments I ever received was from a prophet from Kenya, Africa. He had spoken in our mid-week service the night before. He decided to join our prayer meeting the next morning. After we had prayed for one and a half to two hours that morning, which was normal, he strode over to where I was. He put his finger in my face and said, "You pray like an African." He was commending the passion and life with which we prayed. We weren't there doing a religious exercise. We were there to encounter God and see where it took us. We need these places of participation together in His presence.

The last thing I will mention is we should also demonstrate. Once we learn to pray, we should be able to demonstrate a prayer life in such a way that it inspires others to pray. One of the greatest needs in today's church is a people who know how to pray. This is what happened with Jesus. When the disciples saw His prayer life, it made demands on them. They wanted to do what He knew how to do. May we be a people who inspire, press, and urge others from our place in Him to pray. The truth is, anything and everything God does is first birthed and born from prayer. If there is no prayer there will be no movement. There must be the intercessors who take their place and refuse to stop until His purposes are seen in the earth. Where are the Martin Luthers who said, "I have so much to do that I shall spend the first three hours in prayer"? He was committed to times of seeking the face of God. Nothing was going to get in the way of this time. We must make prayer our priority.

Where are the John Wesleys who said, "God does nothing but in answer to prayer"? Wesley was convinced that if something occurred that was heaven's will, it was a result of someone praying. Nothing just happens. Prayer has to birth it. I believe this with every fiber of my being. Let us be those who pray that the passion of God might be done in the world.

Where are the John Hydes, known as "The Praying Hyde," who went as a missionary to India? So intense was his praying for revival and outpouring that his heart actually moved from the left side of his body to the right. It is reported that:

> "Praying Hyde," as he was called, spent days and nights
> in prayer for an awakening throughout India. In 1904,
> Indian Christians and western missionaries gathered for

the first of an annual series of conventions at Sialkot in what is today Pakistan. John's prayers were answered in a series of outpourings of the Spirit. Often the glory rested on these meetings in a mighty way, while hidden, out of sight, John Hyde and a faithful few travailed in prayer.

John was willing to pay the price and lay down his own life so that God's kingdom could come in power in India. He entered into the sufferings of Christ, dying at the age of 47 from the effects of his intense life of intercession without food or sleep. His heart had moved from its normal position (in the left) to the right. He went home to America and died there, in February 1912. His last words were "Shout the victory of Jesus Christ!"

The Praying Hyde declared, "Give me souls, oh God, or I die." He and his companions through their efforts produced nothing until they gave themselves to prayer. The result was a tremendous move of God sweeping many into the kingdom of God. God is calling many to places of intercession in secret to birth the salvation of multitudes. There are those who clamor for the spotlight of the platform. Where are those who cry out from the place in the spirit realm for Jesus to have what He died for—the souls of men?

Where are the Rees Howells and others who prayed with such tenacity that their prayers are still felt today? Through his prayers a Bible school in Wales was born and used to touch the world through prayer. Mrs. Rees Howells in speaking of her husband's prayer life told Leonard Ravenhill an inside story of what others marveled at.

After I spoke at a session in the Bible School of Wales, Mrs. Rees Howells called me for a private talk. We stood on the veranda of her home overlooking beautiful Swansea Bay. I can see her finger upheld as she said, "Many talk of my husband's buying this place with a shilling (fourteen cents) in his pocket. What they forget is that he prayed twelve hours a day for eleven months to know the mind of God." Brethren, that's discipline! (Ravenhill)

Are there those today who will leave a legacy of prayer that will not only affect this generation but also the ones to come? I hope so. Where are those whom the coming generations will be inspired by, not because of the doctrine they taught or the fame they gained but the prayers they prayed that changed and altered history?

My prayer is that this book on how Jesus taught His disciples to pray will, in a small way, inspire a generation to take their place in the realms of the spirit and see change come to our culture. We can see more accomplished in the spirit dimensions in moments of prayer than we can ever accomplish with years of effort in the natural. May we become a people of His presence and power as we encounter Him in the places of prayer we have been granted access into. He awaits us to come after Him. Will you be one who will? There are amazing realms of the unseen that will greet us when we with childlike faith take Jesus at His word and enter them. God bless you on your pursuit.

ABOUT ROBERT HENDERSON

Robert Henderson is a global apostolic leader who operates in revelation and impartation. His teaching empowers the Body of Christ to see the hidden truths of Scripture clearly and apply them for breakthrough results. Driven by a mandate to disciple nations through writing and speaking, and other forms of media including his show "The Courts of Heaven with Robert Henderson" on GODTV. Robert travels extensively around the globe, teaching on the apostolic, the Kingdom of God, the "Seven Mountains," and, most notably, the Courts of Heaven. He has been married to Mary for over 40 years. They have six children and a growing number of grandchildren. Together they are enjoying life in beautiful Waco, Texas.

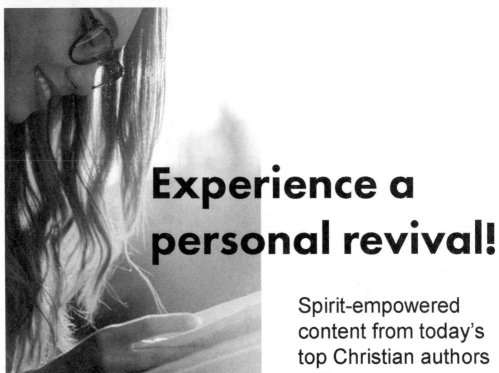